LETTERS FROM M

IN 1915 AND JANUARY, 1916,
FROM ROBERT PALMER, WHO
WAS KILLED IN THE BATTLE OF
UM EL HANNAH, JUNE 21, 1916
AGED 27 YEARS

PRINTED FOR PRIVATE CIRCULATION ONLY

*He went with a draft from the 6th Hants
to reinforce the 4th Hants. The 6th Hants
had been in India since November, 1914.*

British Library Cataloguing-in-Publication Data
A catalogue record for this book is available from the
British Library

Introduction to the

World War One Centenary Series

The First World War was a global war centred in Europe that began on 28 July 1914 and lasted until 11 November 1918. More than nine million combatants were killed, a casualty rate exacerbated by the belligerents' technological and industrial sophistication – and tactical stalemate. It was one of the deadliest conflicts in history, paving the way for major political changes, including revolutions in many of the nations involved. The war drew in all the world's great economic powers, which were assembled in two opposing alliances: the Allies (based on the Triple Entente of the United Kingdom, France and the Russian Empire) and the Central Powers of Germany and Austria-Hungary. These alliances were both reorganised and expanded as more nations entered the war: Italy, Japan and the United States joined the Allies, and the Ottoman Empire and Bulgaria joined the Central Powers. Ultimately, more than 70 million military personnel were mobilised.

The war was triggered by the assassination of Archduke Franz Ferdinand of Austria, heir to the throne of Austria-Hungary, by a Yugoslav nationalist, Gavrilo Princip in Sarajevo, June 28th 1914. This set off a diplomatic crisis when Austria-Hungary delivered an ultimatum to Serbia, and international alliances were invoked. Within weeks, the major powers were at war and the conflict soon spread around the world. By the end of the war, four major imperial powers; the German, Russian, Austro-Hungarian and Ottoman empires—ceased to exist. The map of Europe was redrawn, with several independent nations restored or created. On peace, the League of Nations formed with the aim of preventing any repetition of such an appalling conflict, encouraging cooperation and communication between the newly autonomous nation states. This laudatory pursuit failed spectacularly with the advent of the Second World War however, with new European nationalism and the rise of fascism paving the way for the next global crisis.

This book is part of the World War One Centenary series; creating, collating and reprinting new and old works of poetry, fiction, autobiography and analysis. The series forms a commemorative tribute to mark the passing of one of the world's bloodiest wars, offering new perspectives on this tragic yet fascinating period of human history.

Amelia Carruthers

A Timeline of the Major Events of World War One in Europe

<u>1914</u>

28th June   Franz Ferdinand Assassinated
at Sarajevo.

29th June   Austro-Hungary send despatch to
Vienna accusing Serbian
complicity in the killing.

5th July   Kaiser Wilhelm promises
German support for Austria
against Serbia.

20th July   Austria-Hungary sends
troops to the Serbian frontier.

25th July   Serbia mobilises its troops,
Russia sends troops to the
Austrian frontier.

28th July   Austria-Hungary Declares war
on Serbia.

29th July	Austrians bombard Belgrade and German patrols cross the French border. Britain warns it cannot remain neutral.
1st August	Germany declares war on Russia. Italy and Belgium announce neutrality. French mobilisation ordered.
3rd August	Germany declares war on France and invades Belgium (Schlieffen plan). Great Britain mobilises.
4th August	Britain declares war on Germany and Austria-Hungary (after ultimatum to stand down). US declares neutrality. Germany declares war on Belgium.
6th August	First British casualties with the HMS Amphion sunk by German mines in the North sea. 150 men dead.
7th August	First members of the BEF (British Expeditionary Force) arrive in France.

11th August	Start of enlisting for Kitchener's New Army 'Your King and Country Need You'.
20th August	Brussels is evacuated as German troops occupy the city.
23rd August	The BEF started its retreat from Mons. Germany invades France.
26th August	Russian army defeated at Tannenburg and Masurian Lakes. BEF suffers over 7000 casualties at the Battle of Le Cateau –forced to retreat.
6th September	Battle of the Marne starts; checks German advance, but at the cost of 13,000 British, 250,000 French and 250,000 German casualties.
19th October	First Battle of Ypres.
29th October	Turkey enters the war (on Germany's side).
22nd November	Trenches are now established along the entire Western Front.
8th December	Battle of the Falkland Islands.

1915

19th January	First Zeppelin raid on Britain (Great Yarmouth and Kings Lynn – killing 5).
18th February	Blockade of Great Britain by German U-boats begins. All vessels considered viable targets, including neutrals.
22nd April	Second Battle of Ypres begins. Widespread use of poison gas by Germany.
25th April	Allied troops land in Gallipoli.
2nd May	Austro-German offensive on Galicia begins.
7th May	The Lusitania is sunk by a German U-Boat – creating US/German diplomatic crisis.
23rd May	Italy declares war on Germany and Austria
31st May	First Zeppelin raid on London, killing 35 and shaking morale.

30th June	German troops use flamethrowers for the first time, against the British at Hooge, Ypres.
5th August	Germany captures Warsaw from the Russians.
21st August	Final British offensive in the Dardanelles (Scimitar Hill, Gallipoli). They lose, and suffer 5000 deaths.
25th September	Start of the Battle of Loos and Champagne. The British use gas for the first time, but the wind blows it over their own troops, resulting in 2632 casualties.
31st October	Steel helmets introduced on the British Front.
15th December	Sir Douglas Haig replaces Sir John French as Commander of the BEF.

1916

8th January   Allied evacuation of Helles marks the end of the Gallipoli campaign.

21st February   Start of the Battle of Verdun – German offensive against the Mort-Homme Ridge. The battle lasts 10 months and over a million men become casualties. (Finishes 18th December, the longest and costliest battle of the Western Front).

9th March   Germany declares war on Portugal. Six days later, Austria follows suit.

31st May   Battle of Jutland – lasts until 1st June. German High Seas Fleet is forced to retire despite having inflicted heavier losses on the Royal Navy (14 ships and 6,100 men). German fleet irreparably damaged.

4th June   Start of the Russian Brusilov Offensive on the Eastern front. Nearly cripples Austro-Hungary.

1st July	Start of the Battle of the Somme – 750,000 allied soldiers along a 25 mile front. Nearly 60,000 are dead or wounded on the first day.
14th July	Battle of Bazetin Ridge marks the end of the first Somme Offensive. The British break the German line but fail to deploy cavalry fast enough to take advantage. 9,000 men are lost.
23rd July	Battle of Pozières Ridge marks the second Somme Offensive, costs 17,000 allied casualties – the majority of whom are Australian. (ends 7th August).
10th August	End of the Brusilov Offensive.
9th September	The Battle of Ginchy. The British capture Ginchy – a post of vital strategic importance as it commands a view of the whole battlefield.
15th September	First use en masse of tanks at the Somme. The Battle of Flers-Courcelette signifies the start of the third stage of the Somme offensive.

13th November	Battle of Ancre. The fourth phase of the Somme Offensive is marked by the British capturing Beaumont Hamel and St. Pierre Division, taking nearly 4,000 prisoners.
12th December	Germany delivers Peace Note to Allies suggesting compromise.

1917

1st February	Germany's unrestricted submarine warfare campaign starts.

1st February

Germany's unrestricted submarine warfare campaign starts.

3rd February

US sever diplomatic relations with Germany as U-boats threaten US shipping. Intercepted messages reveal that Germany is provoking the Mexicans into war with the US.

21st February

The great German withdrawal begins. Serre, Miraumont, Petit Miraumont, Pys and Warlencourt are evacuated, falling back 25 miles to establish stronger positions on the Hindenburg Line.

15th March

Tsar Nicholas II abdicates as Moscow falls to Russian Revolutionaries. Demise of the Russian army frees German troops for the Western front.

6th April

USA declares war on Germany – troops mobilise immediately.

9th April	Battle of Arras. British successfully employ new tactics of creeping barrages, the 'graze fuse' and counter battery fire.
16th April	France launches an unsuccessful offensive on the Western Front. – Second Battle of Aisne begins as part of the 'Nivelle Offensive'. Losses are horrendous, triggering mutinies in the French Army.
7th June	The Battle of Messines Ridge. British succeed with few casualties, detonating 19 mines under German front lines – the explosions are reportedly heard from England.
13th June	Germans launch first major heavy bomber raid of London – kills and injures 594.
25th June	First US troops arrive in France.
31st July	Start of the Third Battle at Ypres – a 15 mile front in Flanders. Initial attacks are successful as the German forward trenches are lightly manned.

15th August	The Battle of Lens (Hill 70). – Canadians at the forefront , won a high vantage point, though loss of 9,200 men.
20th August	Third Battle of Verdun begins. French progress is marked by gaining lost territory in the earlier battles.
9th October	The third phase of the Ypres Offensive begins with British and French troops taking Poelcapelle. 25mm of rain falls in 48 hours and the battlefield turns into a quagmire.
12th October	British launch assault at Ypres Against the Passchendale Ridge. New Zealand and Australians take terrible casualties. Bogged down in mud and forced back to start lines.
24th October	Battle of Caporetto – Italian Army heavily defeated.
26th October	Second Battle of Passchendaele begins, 12,000 men lost and 300 yards gained (ends 10th November – 500,000 casualties,

140,000 deaths and 5 miles gained).

6th November

Britain launches major offensive on the Western Front.

20th November

Victory for British tanks at Cambrai - The Royal flying Corps drop bombs at the same time on German anti-tank guns and strong points. Early example of the 'Blitzkrieg' tactics later used by Germany in World War Two.

5th December

Armistice between Germany and Russia signed.

1918

16th January	Riots in Vienna and Budapest with dissatisfaction at the war.
3rd March	Treaty of Brest-Litovsk signed between (Soviet) Russia and Germany.
21st March	Second Battle of the Somme marked by the German spring offensive, the 'Kaiserschlacht'. Germans attack along a 50 mile front south of Arras.
22nd March	Victory for Germany with operation Michael - Use of new 'Storm trooper' assault to smash through British positions west of St. Quentin, taking 16,000 prisoners.
23rd March	Greatest air battle of the war takes place over the Somme, with 70 aircraft involved.
5th April	The German Spring Offensive halts outside Amiens as British and Australian forces hold the Line. The second 1917 battle of

the Somme ends, as Germany calls off operation Michael.

9th April	Germany starts offensive in Flanders –Battle of the Lys (ends 29th April).
19th May	German air force launches largest raid on London, using 33 aircraft.
27th May	Operation Blucher – The Third German Spring Offensive attacks the French army along the Aisne River. French are forced back to the Marne, but hold the river with help from the Americans.
15th July	Second battle of the Marne started; final phase of German spring offensive. Start of the collapse of the German army with irreplaceable casualties.
8th August	Second Battle of Amiens – German resistance sporadic and thousands surrender.
27th September	British offensive on the Cambrai Front leads to the storming of the Hindenburg Line. Battle of St.

Quentin – British and U.S troops launch devastating offensives.

4th October	Germany asks the allies for an armistice (sent to Woodrow Wilson).
8th October	Allies advance along a 20 mile front from St. Quentin to Cambrai, driving the Germans back and capturing 10,000 troops.
29th October	Germany's navy mutinies (at Jade).
3rd November	Austria makes peace. German sailors mutiny at Kiel.
9th November	Kaiser Wilhelm abdicates and revolution breaks out in Berlin.
11th November	Germany signs the armistice with the allies – coming into effect at 11.00am (official end of WWI).

<u>1919</u>

10th January   Communist Revolt in Berlin (Battle of Berlin).

18th January   Paris Peace Conference Begins.

25th January   Principle of a League of Nations ratified.

6th May   Under conditions of the Peace conference, German colonies are annexed.

21st June   The surrendered German naval fleet at Scapa Flow was scuttled.

28th June   Treaty of Versailles signed.

19th July   Cenotaph unveiled in London.

By Amelia Carruthers

Image 1. British troops going on picket --
Mesopotamia

"Up Warwicks! Show the bastards yer-cap badges."

1916: Then Lieutenant. Quoting Private Richard Chuck in the Mesopotamian Campaign.

"There were many words that you could not stand to hear and finally only the names of places had dignity. Abstract words such as glory, honor, courage, or hallow were obscene."

American novelist and WW1 veteran Ernest Hemingway, in 'A Farewell to Arms', 1929

To The Poet Before Battle

Now, youth, the hour of thy dread passion comes;
Thy lovely things must all be laid away;
And thou, as others, must face the riven day
Unstirred by rattle of the rolling drums
Or bugles' strident cry. When mere noise numbs
The sense of being, the sick soul doth sway,
Remember thy great craft's honour, that they may say
Nothing in shame of poets. Then the crumbs
Of praise the little versemen joyed to take
Shall be forgotten; then they must know we are,
For all our skill in words, equal in might
And strong of mettle as those we honoured. Make
The name of poet terrible in just war,
And like a crown of honour upon the fight.

by Ivor Gurney 1917

LETTERS FROM MESOPOTAMIA

War deemed he hateful, for therein he saw Passions unloosed in licence, which in man Are the most evil, a false witness to The faith of Christ. For when by settled plan, To gratify the lustings of the few, The peoples march to battle, then, the law

Of love forgotten, men come out to kill Their brothers in a hateless strife, nor know The cause wherefor they fight, except that they Whom they as rulers own, do bid them so. And thus his heart was heavy on the day That war burst forth. He felt that men could ill

Afford to travel back along the years That they had mounted, toiling, stage by stage— —A year he was to India's plains assigned Nor heard the spite of rifles, nor the rage Of guns; yet pondered oft on what the mind Experiences in war; what are the fears,

And what those joys unknown that men do feel In stress of fight. He saw how great a test Of manhood is a stubborn war, which draws Out all that's worst in men or all that's best: Their fiercest brutal passions from all laws Set free, men burn and plunder, rape and steal;

Or all their human strength of love cries out Against such suffering. And so he came In time to wish that he might thus be tried, Partly to know himself, partly from shame That others with less faith had gladly died, While he in peace and ease had cast a doubt,

Not on his faith, but on his strength to bear So great a trial. Soon it was his fate To test himself; and with the facts of war So clear before him he could feel no hate, No passion was aroused by what he saw, But only pity. And he put all fear

Away from him, terming it the offspring Of an unruly mind. Like some strong man Whom pygmies in his sleep have bound with threads Of twisted cobweb, and he to their plan Is captive while he sleeps, but quickly shreds His bonds when he awakes and sees the thing

That they have bound him with. His faith and will Purged all evil passions from his mind, And left there one great overmastering love For all his fellows. War taught him to find That peace, for which at other times he strove In vain, and new-found friendship did fulfil

His thoughts with happiness. Such was the soul That he perfected, ready for the call Of his dear Master (should it to him come), Scornful of death's terrors, yet withal Loath to leave this life, while still was some Part of the work he dreamed undone, his goal

As yet unreached. There was for such an one A different work among those given, Who've crossed the border of eternity In youthful heedlessness,—as unshriven Naked souls joined the great fraternity O' the dead, while yet their life was just begun ...

And so he went from us unto his task, For all our life is as it were a mask That lifteth at our death, and death is birth To higher things than are upon this earth.

L. P.

Flashman's Hotel,
Rawal Pindi.

April 25th, 1915.

To his Mother.

They are calling for volunteers from Territorial battalions to fill gaps in the Persian Gulf—one subaltern, one sergeant, and thirty men from each battalion. So far they have asked the Devons, Cornwalls, Dorsets, Somersets and East Surreys, but not the Hampshires. So I suppose they are going to reserve us for feeding the 4th Hants in case they want casualties replaced later on. Even if they come to us, I don't think they are likely to take me or Luly, because in every case they are taking the senior subaltern: and that is a position which I am skipping by being promoted along with the three others: and Luly is a long way down the list. But of course I shall volunteer, as there is no adequate reason not to; so I thought you would like to know, only you mustn't worry, as the chance of my going is exceedingly remote: but I like to tell you everything that happens.

Four months after he wrote this, in August, 1915, Robert was on leave at Naini Tal, with Purefoy Causton, a brother officer.

Métropole Hotel,
Naini Tal.

August 3rd, 1915.

To his Mother.

It has been extremely wet since I last wrote. On Saturday we could do nothing except laze indoors and play billiards and Friday was the same, with a dull dinner-party at the end of it. It was very nice and cool though, and I enjoyed those two days as much as any.

On Sunday we left Government House in order to be with Guy Coles during his three days' leave.

It rained all the morning: we went to Church at a spikey little chapel just outside Government House gate. It cleared about noon and we walked down to the Brewery, about three miles to meet Guy. When he arrived we had lunch there and then got ponies.

We had arranged to take Guy straight to a picnic with a nice Mrs. Willmott of Agra, who comes here for the hot weather. So we rode up past the lake and to the very top of Agarpatta, one of the humps on the rim of hills. It took us over two hours, and the mist settled in just as we arrived, about 5, so we picnicked chillily on a misty mountain-top; but Mrs. Willmott and her sister are exceptionally nice people, so we all enjoyed it. They have two small children and a lady nurse for them. I never met one before, but it is quite a sensible plan out here.

We only got back to this Hotel just before dinner, and there I found a wire from Major Wyatt asking me if I would command a draft and take it to the 4th Hants in the Persian Gulf. This is the exact fulfilment of the calculation I wrote to you in April, but it came as a surprise at the moment. I was more excited than either pleased or depressed. I don't hanker after fighting, and I would, of course, have preferred to go with the regiment and not as a draft. But now that I'm in for it, the interest of doing something after all these months of hanging about, and in particular the responsibility of looking after the draft on the way, seems likely to absorb all other feelings. What appeals to me most is the purely unmilitary prospect of being able to protect the men, to some extent, from the, I'm sure, largely preventible sickness there has been in the P.G. The only remark that ever made me feel a sudden desire to go to any front was when O'Connor at Lahore told me (quite untruly as it turned out) that "the Hampshires are dying like flies at Basra." As a matter of fact, they only had ten deaths, but a great deal of sickness, and I do enjoy the prospect of trying to be efficient about that. As for fighting, it doesn't look as if there would be much, whereon Purefoy greatly commiserates me; but if that is the only privation I shan't complain!

I'm afraid your lively imagination will conjure up every kind of horror, and that is the only thing that distresses me about going: but clearly a tropical climate suits me better than most people, and I will be very careful to avoid all unnecessary risks! both for your peace of mind and also to keep the men up to the mark, to say nothing of less exalted motives.

I know no details at all yet. I am to return to Agra on Saturday, so I shall only lose forty-eight hours of my most heavenly fortnight here.

I got this wire Sunday evening and Purefoy sat up talking on my bed till quite late as we had a lot to say to each other.

August 4th. On Monday morning it was pouring harder than ever, quite an inch to the hour. I walked across to the Telegraph Office and answered the Major's wire, and got wet through. After breakfast I chartered a dandy and waded through the deluge to the station hospital, where the M.O. passed me as sound, without a spark of interest in any of my minor ailments. I then proceeded to the local chemist and had my medicine-case filled up, and secured an extra supply of perchloride. There is no Poisons Act here and you can buy perchloride as freely as pepper. My next visit was to the dentist. He found two more decayed teeth and stopped them with incredible rapidity. The climate is so mild that though I was pretty wet through I never felt like catching a cold from being operated on. He was an American with a lady assistant to hold one's mouth open! I never feel sure that these dentists don't just drill a hole and then stop it: but no doubt teeth decay extremely quickly out here.

Then I went back to the Telegraph Office and cabled to Papa and got back in time for lunch after the moistest morning I ever remember being out in.

This hotel is about the worst in the world, I should say, though there are two in Naini reputed to be worse still. It takes in no newspaper, has no writing-paper, only one apology for a sitting-room, and can't supply one with fuel even for a fire. However, Moni Lal is resourceful and we have survived three days of it. Luckily there is an excellent custom here by which visitors belonging to another club, *e.g.,* the Agra Club can join the Naini Club temporarily for 1s. per day. So we spent the afternoon and evening at the Club and I spiflicated both Purefoy (giving him forty and two turns to my one) and Guy at Billiards.

On Tuesday (yesterday) we got up at 7.0 and went for a sail on the lake. Guy is an expert at this difficult art and we circumnavigated the place twice before breakfast with complete success and I learned enough semi-nautical terms to justify the purchase of a yachting cap should occasion arise.

After breakfast we were even more strenuous and climbed up to Government House to play golf. It came on to rain violently just as we arrived, so we waited in the guard-room till it cleared, and then played a particularly long but very agreeable 3-ball, in which I lost to Guy on the last green but beat Purefoy three and one. We got back to lunch at about 3.15.

As if this wasn't enough I sallied out again at 4.0 to play tennis at the Willmotts, quite successfully, with a borrowed racquet, my own having burst on introduction to the climate of this place. Mrs. W. told me that there was a Chaplain, one Kirwan, here just back from the Persian Gulf, so I resolved to pursue him.

I finished up the day by dining P. and G. at the Club, and after dinner Purefoy, by a succession of the most hirsute flukes, succeeded in beating me by ten to his great delight.

I went to bed quite tired, but this morning it was so lovely that I revived and mounted a horse at 7.0 leaving the other two snoring. I rode up the mountain. I was rewarded by a most glorious view of the snows, one of the finest I have ever seen. Between me and them were four or five ranges of lower hills, the deepest richest blue conceivable, and many of their valleys were filled with shining seas of rolling sunlit cloud. Against this foreground rose a quarter-circle sweep of the snows, wreathed and garlanded with cloud wracks here and there, but for the most part silhouetted sharply in the morning sun. The grandest mass was in the centre: Nanda Devi, 25,600, which is the highest mountain in the Empire, and Trisoul, over 22,000. There were six or eight other peaks of over 20,000 ft.

I got back to the Hotel for breakfast, and from 9.30 to 10.45 we played tennis, and then changed hastily and went to Church for the War Anniversary Service. The station turned out for this in unprecedented numbers—churchgoing is not an Anglo-Indian habit—and there was no seat to be had, so I sat on the floor. The Bishop of Lucknow, Foss's uncle, preached.

After the service I waylaid the Revd. Kirwan and found he was staying with the Bishop, who immediately asked us to lunch. So Purefoy and I went to lunch—Guy preferring to sail—and I extracted quite a lot of useful information from K. Incidentally the Bishop showed me a letter from Foss, who wrote from the apex of the Ypres salient. He isn't enjoying it much, I'm afraid, but was quite well.

When we left the Bishop, it was coming out so fine that we decided to ride up and try again to see the snows. So up we rode, and the cloud effects were lovely, both over the plains and among the mountains; but they hid more than half the snows.

We rode down again to Valino's, the nutty tea-shop here, where we had reserved a table on the balcony. Guy was there before us and we sat there till nearly seven listening to the band. We got back to dinner where Purefoy had secured one of his innumerable lightning friends to dine with us, and adjourned to the Club for billiards afterwards: quite a full day.

Thursday: Government House.—Another busy day. It was fine again this morning, so we all three rode up to Snow View and got an absolutely perfect view: the really big snows were clear and cloudless, while the lower slopes and hills and valleys were flooded with broken seas of dazzling cloud. I put it second only to the Darjeeling view.

After breakfast Purefoy and I came up and played golf. Guy took fright at the chance of being asked in to lunch here and went sailing again. A shower made us late in starting, and we only got through twelve holes, after many misfortunes. I ended dormy five.

Lady M. had been in bed ever since we left, but is up to-day, looking rather ill still.

To-night there is a dinner party.

Friday.—The dinner party was uneventful. I sat next a Mrs. ——, one of the silliest females I ever struck. Her only noteworthy remark was that of course the Germans were well equipped for the War as they had been preparing for it for arcades and arcades.

It is wet again to-day. No mail has arrived. I start for Agra after lunch. I have had a delicious holiday. My address now will be:

"Attached 1/4 Hants Regt.,
I.E.F. 'D,' c/o India Office, S.W."

and post a day early.

Naini Tal Club.

August 4th, 1915.

To N.B.

I got a telegram on Sunday asking me to take out a draft to the 4th Hants, in the Persian Gulf, so my address till further notice will be "I.E.F. 'D,' c/o India Office, S.W." I thought I should hate the idea of going to the P.G., but now that it's come along I'm getting rather keen on going. We have been kicking our heels so long while everyone else has been slaving away at the front, that one longs to be doing something tangible and active. The P.G. is not exactly the spot one would select for a pleasure trip: but on the other hand there is likely to be more to do there that is more in my line than the purely military side of the business. The main trouble there is sickness and I'm sure a lot of it is preventible: and though in a battle I should be sure to take the wrong turn and land my detachment in some impossible place, I don't feel it so beyond me to remind them to boil their water and wear their helmets.

I don't know when I'm off, having heard nothing but the bare telegram. They don't want me back in Agra till Saturday, so I shall almost finish my full fortnight's leave. It has been heavenly here and the memory of it will be a joy for months to come. The forests are lovelier than ever: the ferns which clothe the trees are now full grown, and pale purple orchids spangle the undergrowth. Wild dahlias run riot in every open bank, and the gardens are brilliant with lilies and cannas.

It rained with drenching persistence for three days, but the last two have been lovely. I got up early this morning, rode up a mountain and saw the most superb view of the snows. The brown hills between me and the snows had their valleys full of rolling white clouds, and the result was a study in deepest blue and purest white, more wonderful I think than anything I've seen.

The whole station turned out to the Anniversary Service to-day. It is dreadful to think that we've all been denying our Christianity for a whole year and are likely to go on doing so for another. How our Lord's heart must bleed for us! It appals me to think of it.

Government House,
Naini Tal.

August 5th, 1915.

To his Father.

I have written all the news to Mamma this week. The chief item from my point of view is that, as I cabled to you, I am to take a draft from our two Agra Double Coys. to reinforce the 4th Hants, who are now at Nasiriya on the Euphrates. I got the wire asking me to do this on Sunday, but have heard no details since (this is Thursday night), so I presume they know nothing more at Agra or the Major or Luly would surely have written.

On the other hand the Major wants me back in Agra by Saturday, so I suppose I shall be starting some time next week, but unless I hear before posting this I can tell you nothing of the strength or composition of the draft or the date of sailing.

Everyone insists on (α) congratulating me for going to a front and (β) condoling that it is the P.G. I don't really agree with either sentiment. I'm afraid I regard all war jobs as nasty, and the more warlike the nastier, but I do think one ought to taste the same cup as all one's friends are drinking, and if I am to go to any front I would as soon go to the P.G. as anywhere. It will be a new part of the world to me and very interesting. The only bore is being separated from the regiment.

Friday.—I had a talk on Wednesday with a Chaplain just returned from Basra, and he told me we're likely to stand fast now holding the line Nasiriya-Awaz (or some such place on the Tigris). An advance on Baghdad is impossible without two more divisions, because of the length of communications. There is nothing to be gained by advancing to any intermediate point. The only reason we went as far as Nasiriya was that it was the base of the army we beat at Shaiba, and they had reformed there in sufficient strength to be worth attacking. This is not thought likely to happen again, as the Dardanelles will increasingly absorb all Turkey's resources.

It seems to me that what is wanted here pre-eminently is thinking ahead. The moment the war stops unprecedented clamours will begin, and only a Government which knows its aim and has thought out its method can deal with them. It seems to me, though my judgment is fearfully hampered by my inability to get at any comprehensive statement of most of the relevant facts, that the aim may be fairly simply defined, as the training of India to self-government within the Empire, combined with its good administration in trust meanwhile. That gives you a clear criterion—India's welfare, not British interests, and fixes the limit of the employment of Indians as the maximum consistent with good government.

The *method* is of course far more difficult and requires far more knowledge of the facts than I possess. But I should set to work at it on these lines:—

1. Certain qualities need to be developed, responsibility, public spirit, self-respect and so on. This should be aimed at (i) by our own example and teaching, (ii) by a drastic reform of higher education.

2. The barbarisms of the masses must be attacked. This can only be done by a scheme of universal education.

3. The material level of civilisation should be raised. This means agricultural and industrial development, in which technical education would play a large part.

Therefore, your method may be summed up in two words, sympathy and education. The first is mainly, of course, a personal question. Therefore, preserve at all costs a high standard of *personnel* for I.C.S. Try to get imaginative men at the top. Let all ranks understand from the outset the aim they have to work for, and let Indians know it. Above all let every official act prove it, confidence is a plant of slow and tender growth here. Beware of phrases and western formulæ; probably the benevolent autocrat, whether English or Indian, will always govern better than a committee or an assembly.

The second—education—is a question of £ *s. d.* The aim should be a far-sighted and comprehensive scheme. A great effort to get the adequate funds should be made and a scheme capable of ready expansion started. Reform of higher education will be very unpopular, but should be firmly and thoroughly carried out; it ought not to cost much. The bulk of the money at first should go to technical education and the encouragement of agriculture and industry. This will be remunerative, by increasing the country's wealth. Elementary education would have to begin by supplying schools where asked for, at a certain rate. From this they would aim at making it gradually universal, then free, then compulsory. But that will be many years hence inevitably.

I should work at a policy on these lines: announce it, invite Indian co-operation, and meanwhile deal very firmly with all forms of disorder.

Agra.

August 12th, 1915.

To R.K.

This last list is almost more than I can bear. It is hardly possible to think of poor dear Gilbert as killed. Do let me know how Foss is and how he gets on. Your letters are such a joy, and they give me news I get from nobody else.

I'm afraid my share in the correspondence may become even less than before, as I shall henceforth be on more than nominally active service and under the eye of the censor.

Luly is clamouring for lunch, which we eat at 11, and I shall have no peace afterwards till the ship reaches a landlocked bit of Gulf: so goodbye for the present.

"S.S. Varsova,"
Bombay.

August 16th, 1915.

To his Mother.

I shall just have time to write you a line about our journey so far, and may be able to write to Papa later.

They gave me a very nice farewell dinner on Friday at Agra. Raju came and sat next me and it all went off very well. Almost the whole station turned up. After dinner we sat outside, playing the gramophone, etc. Swift, seconded by Luly and Purefoy, made a determined effort to make me tight by standing me drinks and secretly instructing the Khitmagar to make them extra strong; but I was not quite green enough for that and always managed to exchange drinks at the last moment with the result that Swift got pretty tight and I didn't.

I sat in the bungalow talking to Purefoy till 2, and was up again at 6. From 6 till 11 I was busy with seeing to things and hardly had a moment's peace. We paraded at 10.45 and marched to the station, with the Punjabis band leading us. It was excessively warm for marching orders—96° in the shade—and the mile to the station was quite enough. There a great crowd on the platform and everyone was very nice and gave us a splendid send-off. I was too busy all the time to feel at all depressed at leaving Luly and Purefoy, which I had rather feared I should. Partings are, I think, much more trying in the prospect than at the actual moment, because beforehand the parting fills one's imagination, whereas at the moment one's hopes of meeting again come into active play. Anyway, I hadn't time to think much about it then, and I was already very sleepy. We started at 12.5.

At 1.30 Sergt. Pragnell came running along to say that L/C. Burgess was taken very bad; so I went along, with the Eurasian Assistant-Surgeon, who was travelling with us to Bombay. (These Eurasian A.-S.'s are far more competent than the British R.A.M.C. officers, in my experience.) We found Burgess with all the symptoms of heat-stroke, delirium and red face and hot dry skin. A thermometer under his armpit, after half a minute, showed a temperature of 106°. So the A.S. had all his clothes removed and laid him on a bench in the draught and dabbled him gently with water all over from the water-bottles. Apparently in these cases there are two dangers, either of which proves fatal if not counteracted: (1) the excessive temperature of the body. This rises very rapidly. In another half an hour it would have been 109°, and 110° is generally fatal. This he reduced, by the sponging and evaporation, to about 100° in the course of an hour. But the delirium continued, because (2) the original irritation sends a rush of blood to the head, causing acute congestion, which if it continues produces apoplexy. To prevent this we wanted ice, and I had wired on to Gwalior for some, but that was three hours ahead. Luckily at about 3 we halted to let the mail pass, and a railway official suggested stopping it. This we did, I got some ice which soon relieved the situation. But of course we couldn't take poor Burgess with us, so we wired for an ambulance to meet us at Jhansi, and put him ashore.

Meanwhile at Gwalior a pleasant surprise was in store. We had "train rations" on the usual measly Indian scale, but for tea on Saturday we were to rely on tea provided by Scindia at Gwalior. Happily a Maharajah's ideas of tea are superior to a Quartermaster's, and this is what we had for fifty men! Unlimited tea, with sugar, twenty-five tinned cheeses, fifty tins of sausages and twenty-five 2lb. tins of Marie biscuits! This feed tinted the rest of the journey rose-colour.

The only other incident was the loss by one of the men of his haversack, which he dropped out of window.

Yesterday, Sunday, was much cooler. When I woke at Bhopal it was only 76° and it only got even as high as 89° for about half-an-hour. We ran into rain in the afternoon.

We reached Bhusawal at 7 p.m. and had to wait four hours to be picked up by the Nagpur mail. In the refreshment room I met a Terrier gunner officer who was P.M.C. of the Mess at Barrackpore when we messed there in December. He was just back from a course at Mhow and had been positively told by the Staff Officers there that his and most other T. batteries were to be sent back to Europe in a month's time: and moreover that a whole division of Ts. was going to the Persian Gulf and another to E. Africa.

The air is full of such rumours. Here the Embarkation N.C.O. says 78,000 K's have already sailed to relieve us. But the mere number of the rumours rather discredits them. And the fact of their using us for drafts to P.G. seems to show they don't intend moving the units.

We left Bhusawal at midnight and arrived here at 9.15 without incident. Bombay is its usual mild and steamy self, an unchanging 86°, which seemed hot in November, but quite decently cool now.

This boat is, from the officers' point of view, far more attractive than the "Ultonia." Being a B.I. boat it is properly equipped for the tropics and has good 1st class accommodation. She is about 6,000 tons. The men are, I'm afraid, rather crowded. There will be 1,000 on board when complete. We pick up some at Karachi. We sail to-morrow morning. If not too sea-sick I will write to Papa and post it at Karachi.

I am going out now to do a little shopping and get my hair cut, and I shall post this in the town.

P.S.—The whole country is deliciously green now, not a brown patch except the freshest ploughed pieces, and the rivers no longer beggarly trickles in a waste of rubble, but pretty pastoral streams with luxuriant banks.

"S.S. Varsova,"

*August 21st,*1915.

To N.B.

I don't know when I shall next get one of your letters. It will have to follow me painfully round *via* Agra. And if I post this at Basra, it will have to go back to Bombay before starting for England; though people here are already talking of the time when we shall have finished the Baghdad Railway and letters come by rail from England to Basra in about 5 days.

Meanwhile as I have no letters of your's to answer and no news to discuss, I will try and give you an account of myself and my fifty veterans since I last wrote.

The fifty just form a platoon. You see, my retromotion goes on apace. A Company Commander from August to April, a Company Second in Command from May to August, and now a platoon Commander. I shall find the stage of Sergeant harder still to live up to if it comes to that.

Twenty-five are from 'D' Double Company; but only seven of these are from my own original lambs of 'F': because they wouldn't take anyone under twenty-three, and as I have mentioned before, I think, very few of 'F' have qualified for pensions. As it is, two of the seven gave false ages. The other twenty-five are from a Portsmouth Company—townees mostly, and to me less attractive than the village genius: but I daresay we shall get on all right.

Our start wasn't altogether auspicious—in fact taking a draft across the middle East is nearly as difficult to accomplish without loss as taking luggage across Scotland. We had a very good send-off, and all that— concert, dinner, band, crowd on the platform and all the moral alcohol appropriate to such occasions. It was a week ago, to-day, when we left Agra, and Agra climate was in its top form, 96° in the shade and stuffy at that. So you can imagine that it was not only our spirits that were ardent after a mile's march to the station in marching order at noon. An hour after the train had started one of my lance-corporals collapsed with heat-stroke. The first-aid treatment by the Eurasian M.O. travelling with us was a most instructive object lesson. The great thing is to be in time. We were summoned within ten minutes of the man's being taken ill. His temperature was already 106°: the M.O. said that in another half-hour it would have been 109° and in an hour he would probably have been dead. We stripped him stark, laid him in the full draught, and sponged him so as to produce constant evaporation: held up the Punjab mail and got 22lbs. of ice to put under his head: and so pulled him round in less than two hours. We had to leave him at Jhansi though, and proceeded to Bombay forty-nine strong.

The ten-little-nigger-boy process continued at Bombay. We arrived on board on Monday morning: and though orders were formally issued that nobody was to leave the docks without a pass, no attempt was made to prevent the men spending the day in the town, which they all did.

On the Tuesday morning the crew told the men we should not be sailing till Wednesday: and accordingly a lot of them went shopping again. But for once in a way the ship actually sailed at the appointed time, 11 a.m. on Tuesday, and five of my gallant band were left behind. However they were collected by the Embarkation Authorities, and together with their fellow-victims of nautical inaccuracy from the other drafts were sent up by special train to Karachi, where they rejoined us: the C.O. according them a most unsympathetic reception, and sentencing them all (rather superfluously) to Confinement to Barracks for the remainder of the voyage.

There are no fewer than forty-one units on board this ship. They include drafts from almost every Territorial Battalion in India, convalescents rejoining the regular battalions already in Mesopotamia, and various engineers and gunners. The ship is grossly overcrowded—1,200 on board an ordinary 6,000 ton liner. The officers are very well off, though. She is a bran-new boat, built for this very run (in anticipation of the Baghdad Railway), with big airy cabins and all the latest improvements in lights, fans and punkahs. There is nobody I know on board and though they are quite a pleasant lot they don't call for special comment. The C.O. is a genial major of the Norfolks. He did some star turns the first two days. There was a heavy monsoon swell on, and the boat rolled so, you could hardly stand up. However the Major, undaunted, paraded about a score of men who had squeaked on to the ship after the roll-call at Bombay. These were solemnly drawn up in a line as defaulters and magisterially called to attention to receive judgment. On coming to attention they over-balanced with the regularity of ninepins in a row: and after three attempts the major had to harangue them standing (nominally) at ease. Even so, his admonition was rather impaired by his suddenly sitting down on the deck, and having to leave rather hurriedly for his cabin before the peroration was complete.

We are just going through the Straits of Ormuz now: we saw the coast of Persia on and off all to-day. We spent Thursday, by the bye, at Karachi, an awful hole it looks—treeless and waterless and very much the modern port. It reminds one strongly of Port Said, though not *quite* so repulsive: and there is a touch of Suez thrown in.

So far it has been quite cool, 84 to 86°: but we shall be beyond the cloud-zone to-morrow and right inside the Gulf, so I expect it will get hot now.

We expect to reach Basra on Tuesday evening. After that our movements are wholly unknown to us.

The casualty lists just before we left were so dreadful that I am rather dreading the moment when we see the next batch.

"H.M.S. Varsova,"
Off Fars Is.

August 22, 1915.

To R.K.

It is too warm to be facetious, and I have no letter of yours to answer: so you will have to put up with a bald narrative of our doings since I last wrote.

They gave us various binges at Agra before we left. A concerted effort to make me tight failed completely: in fact of the plotters it could be said that in the same bet that they made privily were their feet taken.

We left on Saturday, 15th: fifty rank and file and myself. One had a heat-stroke almost as soon as the train had started (result of marching to the station at noon in marching order and a temperature of 96°) and we had an exciting hour in keeping his temperature below 109° till we met the mail and could get some ice. We succeeded all right and sent him safely to hospital at Jhansi. The rest of the journey was cooler and uneventful.

We reached Bombay at 9.15 a.m. on Monday, and went straight on board. The ship did not sail till next day and when it did they contrived to leave thirty-two men behind, including five of mine.

This is a new and pleasant boat, almost 6,000 tons and fitted up with every contrivance for mitigating heat. But there are far too many persons on board: nearly 1,200: and as they simply can't breathe between decks, the decks are as crowded as a pilgrim ship's. There are over forty units represented: including drafts from about twenty-eight T.F. battalions.

We had the devil of a swell the first two days, though luckily we hit off a break in the monsoon. Anyway, Mothersibb preserved me from sea-sickness: but in every other respect I felt extremely unwell. We reached Karachi on the Thursday morning and stayed there all day. It is a vile spot, combining the architectural features of a dock with the natural amenities of a desert. The only decent spot was a Zoo and even that had a generally super-heated air.

The thirty-two lost sheep turned up at Karachi, having been forwarded by special train from Bombay. No fatted calf was killed for them: in fact they all got fourteen days C.B. and three days pay forfeited; though, as Dr. Johnson observed, the sea renders the C.B. part rather otiose.

All Friday we coasted along Baluchistan and Persia. It is surprising how big a country Persia is: it began on Friday and goes right up into Europe. On Saturday we reached the Straits of Ormuz and to-day (Sunday) we are well inside the Gulf, as the mention of Fars doubtless conveyed to you.

It is getting pronouncedly hotter every hour. It was a quarter to one when I began this letter and is now half-past twelve, which is the kind of thing that is continually happening. Anyway the bugle for lunch has just gone, and it is 96° in my cabin. I have spent the morning in alternate bouts of bridge and Illingworth on Divine Immanence: I won Rs three at the former: but I feel my brain is hardly capable of further coherent composition until nourishment has been taken. So goodbye for the present. It will take ages for this to reach you.

"P.S.S. Karadeniz,"
Basra.

Friday, August 27th, 1915.

To his Mother.

I wrote to Papa from just outside the bar, which is a mud-bank across the head of the Gulf, about seventeen miles outside Fao. We anchored there to await high tide, and crossed on Tuesday morning.

Fao is about as unimpressive a place as I've seen. The river is over a mile wide there, but the place is absolutely featureless. In fact all the way up it is the same. The surrounding country is as flush with the river as if it had been planed down to it. On either side runs a belt of date palms about half a mile wide, but these are seldom worth looking at, being mostly low and shrubby, like an overgrown market garden.

Beyond that was howling desert, not even picturesquely sandy, but a dried up marsh overblown with dust, like the foreshore of a third-rate port. The only relief to the landscape was when we passed tributaries and creeks, each palm-fringed like the river. Otherwise the only notable sights were the Anglo Persian

Oil Works, which cover over a hundred acres and raised an interesting question of comparative ugliness with man and nature in competition, and a large steamer sunk by the Turks to block the channel and, needless to add, not blocking it.

There was a stiff, warm wind off the desert, hazing the air with dust and my cabin temperature was 100°. Altogether it was rather a depressing entrée, since amply atoned for so far as Nature is concerned.

We reached Basra about 2 p.m. and anchored in midstream, the river being eight hundred yards or so wide here. The city of Basra is about three miles away, up a creek, but on the river there is a port and native town called Ashar.

The scene on the river is most attractive, especially at sunrise and sunset. The banks rise about ten feet from the water: the date palms are large and columnar; and since there is a whole series of creeks, parallel and intersecting—they are the highways and byeways of the place—the whole area is afforested and the wharves and bazaars are embowered in date groves. The river front and the main creeks are crowded with picturesque craft, the two main types being a large high prowed barge, just what I picture to have taken King Arthur at his Passing, but here put to the prosaic uses of heavy transport and called a mahila; and a long darting craft which can be paddled or punted and combines the speed of a canoe with the grace of a gondola and is called, though why I can't conceive, a bhellum. Some of the barges are masted and carry a huge and lovely sail, but the ones in use for I.E.F.D. are propelled by little tugs attached to their sides and quite invisible from beyond, so that the speeding barges seem magically self-moving.

Ashore one wanders along raised dykes through a seemingly endless forest of pillared date palms, among which pools and creeks add greatly to the beauty, though an eyesore to the hygienist. The date crop is just ripe and ripening, and the golden clusters are immense and must yield a great many hundred dates to the tree. When one reaches the native city the streets are unmistakably un-Indian, and strongly reminiscent of the bazaar scene in Kismet. This is especially true of the main bazaar, which is a winding arcade half a mile long, roofed and lined with shops, thronged with men. One sees far fewer women than in India, and those mostly veiled and in black, while the men wear long robes and cloakes and scarves on their heads bound with coils of wool worn garland-wise, as one sees in Biblical pictures. They seem friendly, or rather wholly indifferent to one, and I felt at times I might be invisible and watching an Arabian

Nights' story for all the notice they took of me. By the way, I want you to send me a portable edition of the Arabian Nights as my next book, please.

But the most fascinating sight of all is Ashar Creek, the main thoroughfare, as crowded with boats as Henley at a regatta. The creek runs between brick embankments, on which stand a series of Arabian cafes, thronged with conversational slow moving men who sit there smoking and drinking coffee by the thousand.

It is a wonderful picture from the wooden bridge with the minaret of a mosque and the tops of the tallest date palms for a background.

So much for Ashar: I've not seen Basra city yet. We're here till Sunday probably, awaiting our river boats. There were not enough available to take us all up on Wednesday, so those who are for the front line went first. They have gone to a spot beyond Amara, two-thirds of the way to Kut-al-Amara, which is where the Shatt-al-Hai joins the Tigris. The Shatt-al-Hai is a stream running from the Tigris at K-al-A to the Euphrates at Nasria, and that line is our objective. There is likely to be a stiff fight for the K-al-A, they say, rather to my surprise. But the 4th Hants has been moved to Amara and put on line of communication for the present; so our thirst for bloodshed is not likely to be gratified.

We have moved across to this ship while awaiting our river boat. They use ships here as barracks and hotels, very sensibly seeing that there are none fit for habitation on land; while being about 400 yards from either bank we are practically free from mosquitoes. But this particular ship is decidedly less desirable for residential purposes than the Varsova. It was originally a German boat and was sold to the Turks to be used for a pilgrim ship to Mecca; and I can only conclude either that the Turkish ideas of comfort are very different to ours or that the pilgrimage has a marked element of asceticism.

But I am quite ready to put up with the amenities of a Turkish pilgrim ship. What does try me is the murderous folly of military authorities. They wouldn't let us take our spine-pads from Agra, because we should be issued with them here. They have none here and have no idea when they will get any. Incidentally, no one was expecting our arrival here, least of all the 4th Hants. Everyone says a spine-pad is a necessary precaution here, so I am having fifty made and shall try and make the Colonel pay for them. Every sensible Colonel made his draft stick to theirs; but our's wouldn't let us take them, because Noah never wore one.

To continue the chapter of incredible muddles; the 780 who went off on Wednesday were embarked on their river-boat—packed like herrings—at 9 a.m. and never got started till 4 p.m. A bright performance, but nothing to our little move. This boat is 600 yards from the Varsova, and they had every hour in the twenty-four to choose from for the move. First they selected 2 p.m. Wednesday as an appropriate hour! It was 100° in the shade by 1 p.m., so the prospect was not alluring. At 1.30 the order was washed out and for the rest of the day no further orders could be got for love or money.

We were still in suspense yesterday morning, till at 8.30—just about the latest time for completing a morning movement—two huge barges appeared with orders to embark on them at 10! Not only that, but although there are scores of straw-roofed barges about, these two were as open as row boats, and in fact exactly like giant row boats. To complete the first situation, the S. and S. had not been apprised of the postponement, and so there was no food for the men on board. Consequently they had to load kits, etc., and embark on empty stomachs.

Well, hungry but punctual, we embarked at 10 a.m. It was 102° in my cabin, so you can imagine what the heat and glare of 150 men in an open barge was. Having got us into this enviable receptacle, they proceeded to think of all the delaying little trifles which might have been thought of any time that morning. One way and another they managed to waste three-quarters of an hour before we started. The journey took six minutes or so. Getting alongside this ship took another half hour, the delay mainly due to Arab incompetence this time. Then came disembarking, unloading kits and all the odd jobs of moving units—which all had to be done in a furnace-like heat by men who had had no food for twenty hours. To crown it all, the people on board here had assumed we should breakfast before starting and not a scrap of food was ready. The poor men finally got some food at 2 p.m. after a twenty-two hours fast and three hours herded or working in a temperature of about 140°. Nobody could complain of such an ordeal if we'd been defending Lucknow or attacking Shaiba, but to put such a strain on the men's health—newly arrived and with no pads or glasses or shades—gratuitously and merely by dint of sheer hard muddling—is infuriating to me and criminal in the authorities—a series of scatter-brained nincompoops about fit to look after a cocker-spaniel between them.

Considering what they went through, I think our draft came off lightly with three cases of heat-stroke. Luckily the object lesson in the train and my sermons thereon have borne fruit, and the men acted promptly and sensibly as soon as the patients got bad. Two began to feel ill on the barge and the third became delirious quite suddenly a few minutes after we got on board here. When I arrived on the scene they had already got him stripped and soused, though in the stuffy 'tween decks. I got him up on deck (it was stuffy enough there) and we got ice, and thanks to their promptness, he was only violent for about a quarter of an hour and by the time my kit was reachable and I could get my thermometer, an hour or so later, he was normal. There was no M.O. on board, except a grotesque fat old Turk physician to the Turkish prisoners, whose diagnosis was in Arabic and whose sole idea of treatment was to continue feeling the patient's pulse (which he did by holding his left foot) till we made him stop.

The other two were gradual cases and being watered and iced in time never became delirious; so we may get off without any permanent casualties; but they have taken a most useful corporal and one private to hospital, which almost certainly means leaving them behind on Sunday.

The other men were all pretty tired out and I think it does credit to their constitutions they stood it so well.

I, having my private spine-pad and glasses, was comparatively comfortable, also I had had breakfast and didn't have to shift kits or even my own luggage. I don't dislike even extreme heat nearly as much as quite moderate cold.

I gather it doesn't get so cold here as I thought. 37° is the lowest temperature I've heard vouched for.

I haven't time nowadays to write many letters, so I'm afraid you must ask kind aunts, etc., to be content with parts of this; I hope *they'll* go on writing to *me* though.

"P.S.S. Kara Deuiz,"
Basra,

August 29, 1915.

To N.B.

I hope you will be indulgent if I write less regularly now: and by indulgent I mean that you will go on writing to me, as I do enjoy your letters so much. I expect I shall have slack times when there will be plenty of leisure to write: but at others we are likely to be busy, and you never can be sure of having the necessary facilities. And personally I find my epistolary faculties collapse at about 100° in the shade. I wrote quite happily this morning till it got hot; and only now (4.45) have I found it possible to resume. We get it 102 to 104° every day from about noon to four, and it oppresses one much more than at Agra as there is no escaping from it and flies are plentiful: but about now a nice breeze springs up, and the evenings are fairly pleasant. I thought we were leaving for Amarah to-day, so I told Mama my letter to her would have to do all-round duty, which is mean, I admit, but I had no day off till to-day.

Not that I've been really busy, but I've been out a lot, partly getting things and partly seeing the place.

I've just heard I must go ashore with another sick man immediately after evening service (the Bishop of Lahore is coming on board), so I shall have to cut this measly screed very short. We load kits on our river-boat at 7 a.m. to-morrow and start sometime afterwards for Amarah. My letter to Mama will give you such news as there is. Since writing it I've seen Basra city, which is disappointing, less picturesque than Ashar: also the Base Hospital, which strikes me very favourably, the first military hospital that has: Dum Dum wasn't bad.

We have a lot of Turkish prisoners on board here, and the Government is trying the experiment of letting them out on parole and paying them Rs 10/- a week so long as they report themselves. It is a question whether the result will be to cause the whole Turkish army to surrender, or whether their desire to prolong the war will make the released ones keep their parole a secret. I daresay it will end in a compromise, half the army to surrender and the other half to receive Rs 5/- a week from the surrendered ones to fight on to the bitter end.

I must go and dress for Church parade.

To P.C., *September, 1915.*

"I believe that if I could choose a day of heavy fighting of any kind I liked for my draft, I should choose to spend a day in trenches, under heavy fire without being able to return it. The fine things of war spring from your chance of being killed: the ugly things from your chance of killing."

September, 1915.

To the Same.

"I wonder how long H——'s 'delirious joy' at going to the front will last. Those who have seen a campaign here are all thoroughly converted to my view of fronts. I can't imagine a keener soldier than F——, and even he says he doesn't care if he never sees another Turk, and as to France, you might as well say, 'Hurrah, I'm off to Hell.' Pat M—— goes as far as to say that no sane fellow ever has been bucked at going to the front, as distinguished from being anxious to do his duty by going there. But I don't agree with him. Did you see about the case of a Captain in the Sikhs, who deserted from Peshawar, went to England, enlisted as a private under an assumed name, and was killed in Flanders? The psychology of that man would be very interesting to analyse. It can't have been sense of duty, because he knew he was flagrantly violating his duty. Nor can you explain it by some higher call of duty than his duty as a Sikh Officer, like the duty which makes martyrs disobey emperors. It must have been just the primitive passion for a fight. But if it *was* that, to indulge it was a bad, weak and vicious thing to do. Yet it clearly wasn't a selfish thing to do: on the contrary, it was heroic. He deliberately sacrificed his rank, pay, and prospects and exposed himself to great danger. Still, as far as I can see, he only did it because his passion for fighting was stronger than every other consideration, and therefore he seems to me to be morally in the same class as the man who runs away with his neighbour's wife, or any other victim of strong (and largely noble) passions. And I believe that the people who say they are longing to be at the front can be divided into three classes (1) those who merely say so because it is the right thing to say, and have never thought or wished about it on their own. (2) Those who deliberately desire to drink the bitterest cup that they can find in these times of trouble. These men *are* heroes, and are the men who in peace choose a mission to lepers. (3) The savages, who want to indulge their primitive passions. Perhaps one ought to add as the largest class (4) those who don't imagine what it is like, who think it will be exciting, seeing life, an experience, and so on, and don't think of its reality or meaning at all."

Amara.

Thursday, September 2nd, 1915.

To his Mother.

I only had time to scrawl a short note last night before the mail went. But I wrote to Papa the day before we left Basra.

Our embarkation was much more sensibly managed this time, a Captain Forrest of the Oxfords being O.C. troops, and having some sense, though the brass hats again fixed 10 a.m. as the hour. However he got all our kits on the barge at 7 and then let the men rest on the big ship till the time came. Moreover the barge was covered. We embarked on it at 9.30 and were towed along to the river steamer "Malamir," to which we transferred our stuff without difficulty as its lower deck was nearly level with the barge. The only floater was that my new bearer (who is, I fear, an idiot) succeeded in dropping my heavy kit bag into the river, where it vanished like a stone. Fortunately that kind of thing doesn't worry me much; but while I was looking for an Arab diver to fish for it it suddenly re-appeared the other side of the boat, and was retrieved.

These river boats are flat-bottomed and only draw six feet. They have two decks and an awning, and there was just room for our 200 men to lie about. Altogether there were on board—in the order of the amount of room they took up—two brass hats, 220 men (four

Hants drafts and some odds and ends), a dozen officers, four horses and a dozen native servants and a crew.

Altogether I had to leave four sick men at Basra, all due more or less to that barge episode, and I have still two sickish on my hands, while two have recovered.

There was a strong head-wind and current so we only made about four or five knots an hour. The river is full of mud banks, and the channel winds to and fro in an unexpected manner, so that one can only move by daylight and then often only by constant sounding. Consequently, starting at noon on Monday, it took us till 5 p.m. Wednesday to do the 130 miles. It is much less for a crow, but the river winds so, that one can quite believe Herodotus's yarn of the place where you pass the same village on three consecutive days. Up to Kurna, which we reached at 7 a.m. Tuesday, the river is about 500 yards to 300 yards broad, and the country mainly poor, bare, flat pasture; the date fringe diminishing and in places altogether disappearing for miles together. At the water's edge, as it recedes, patches of millet had been and were being planted. The river is falling rapidly and navigation becomes more difficult every week.

Kurna is aesthetically disappointing. The junction of the rivers is unimpressive, and the place itself a mere quayside and row of mud houses among thin and measly palms. It is of course the traditional site of Eden.

Above Kurna the river is not only halved in width, as one would expect, but narrows rapidly. Most of the day it was only a hundred yards wide and by evening only 60; and of the sixty only a narrow channel is navigable and that has a deep strong current which makes the handling of the boat very difficult.

In the afternoon we passed Ezra's Tomb, which has a beautiful dome of blue tiles, which in India one would date Seventeenth Century. Otherwise it looked rather "kachcha" and out of repair, but it makes an extremely picturesque group, having two clumps of palms on either side of an otherwise open stretch of river.

Soon afterwards we came to a large Bedouin Village, or rather camp, running up a little creek and covering quite fifteen acres. They can't have been there long, as the whole area was under water two months ago. Their dwellings are made of reeds, a framework of stiff and pliant reeds and a covering of reed-matting; the whole being like the cover of a van stuck into the ground and one end closed; but smaller, about 5ft. × 4ft. × 7ft. There were about 100 of these and I should put the population at 700.

A whole crowd of boys and some men came out and ran along with us, and dived in for anything we threw overboard. They swam like ducks of course. All the boys and most of the men were quite naked, which is a thing you never see in India. Any boy over twelve there has a loin-cloth. There seemed to be very few men about: a lot of women came to the doors of their huts. They made no attempt to veil their faces, which even the beggar women in Basra did. Only one girl and one woman ran with the boat; the girl dived with the best; the woman was dressed and her function was to carry the spoils. Incidentally our men discovered a better use for their ration biscuits than attempting to eat them. They made excellent ducks and drakes on the water and the swimmers were quite keen on them. I must say they tasted rather musty besides being very hard, but I think the men chiefly objected to a very small brown beetle which was abundant in them.

When the sun got low we tied up to the bank for twenty minutes and a good many of the men had a bathe; but owing to the current we had to make them keep within a yard or two of the bank.

Next morning, Wednesday, a half-gale was blowing against us and progress was slower than ever. The river got wider again, nearly 200 yards in places, and the wind lashed it into waves. It was a great bore, because you couldn't put anything down for a second. Also three days confined to a minute deck-space made me rather bilious.

In the afternoon the wind blew us ashore when we were in sight of Amara, and it took nearly half an hour to get us off again. Finally, we arrived here about 5 p.m.

This is a town of about 10,000 inhabitants, on the left bank of the Tigris. On the river front is a quay about a mile long, and an equally long row of continental-looking houses. It almost reminds one of Dieppe at moments. The river is about 150 yards wide, and on the other side there are hardly any houses, just a narrow fringe of dates and some fields. All the inhabitants of the river-front have been turned out and it is occupied with offices, stores, hospitals and billets. We occupy a block of four houses, which have a common courtyard behind them, a great cloistered yard, which makes an admirable billet for the men.

We officers live in two of the houses, the third is Orderly Room, etc., and the fourth is used by some Native Regiment Officers. There is no furniture whatever, so it is like camping with a house for a tent. We sleep on the roof and live on the verandahs of the little inner courts. It is decidedly cooler than Basra, and last night I wanted a blanket before dawn for the first time since April (excluding the Hills, of course). In my room now (2.45 p.m.) it is 96° but there is plenty of breeze about.

It seems to be just a chance when the mail goes out: I hope to write to Papa later on in the week and give him the news of this place and the regiment. If I spell names of places without a capital letter it will be for an obvious reason. Also note that the place which is marked on the map Kut-al-Amara is always referred to here as Kut.

P.S.—In regard to what you say about the ducks, I'm told that teal are common in Turkey and snipe in Arabia, but not so common as mallard in England or pintail in India. The bitterns here boom just like guns.

Att. 1/4 Hants,
I.E.F. "D,"
C/o India Office, S.W.

Amarah, *September 4th*,1915.

To R.K.

Yours from Albemarle Street reached me just before we

left Basra. It gave me the first news of Charles Lister's second wound. We get almost no news here. Potted *Reuter* is circulated most days, but each unit may only keep it half an hour, so its two to one against one's seeing it. My only resource is the *Times* which laboriously dogs my steps from England: but it has already been pinched en route four times, so I can't rely on seeing even that: therefore in the matter of casualties, please be as informative as you can, regardless of originality.

As I told you in my last letter that I was going to Nasiriyah, it won't surprise you to find I've got here instead. We reached Basra (it would be much nicer to spell it Bassorah, but I can't be bothered to) on the feast of St. Bartholomew, which the Military call 24/8/15. Considering what places are like out here, B. is wonderfully attractive and picturesque. At least Ashar is, which is the port; Beroea: Corinth:: Ashar: Basra. To begin with it stands between six and eight feet above the river level, an almost unique eminence. Then lots of major and minor creeks branch out from the river and from the main streets. All round and in every unbuilt on space are endless groves of date palms, with masses of yellow dates. The creeks are embanked with brick and lined with popular café's where incredible numbers of Arabs squat and eat or drink huggas and hacshish and the like. The creeks and river swarm with bhellums and mahilas. A bhellum is a cross between a gondola and a Canada canoe: and a mahila is a barge like the ones used by King Arthur, Elaine or the Lady of Shallott: and its course and destination are generally equally vague.

We stayed six days at B. mainly on a captured Turkish pilgrim ship. I suggest a Turkish pilgrimage as a suitable outlet for the ascetic tendencies of your more earnest spikelets. It was hot, but nothing fabulous. My faithful thermometer never got beyond 104 in my cabin. The disadvantage of any temperature over 100 indoors is that the fan makes you hotter instead of cooler. There are only two ways of dealing with this difficulty. One is to drink assiduously and keep an evaporation bath automatically going: but on this ship the drinks used to give out about 4 p.m. and when it comes to neat Tigris-cum-Euphrates, I prefer it applied externally. So I used to undress at intervals and sponge all over and then stand in front of the fan. While you're wet it's deliciously cool: as soon as you feel the draught getting warm, you dress again and carry on. This plan can't be done here as there are no fans. I suppose you realised that Austen Chamberlain was only indulging his irrepressible sense of humour when he announced in the H. of C. that in Mesopotamia "The health of troops has on the whole been good. Ice and fans are installed wherever possible," *i.e.* nowhere beyond Basra. The hot weather sickness casualties have been just over 30% of the total force: but as they were nearly all heat-stroke and malaria, it ought to be much better now. Already the nights are cool enough for a blanket to be needed just before dawn. Of course they run up the sick list by insane folly. When we moved to our Turkish ship there was every hour of the day or night to choose from to do it in, and plenty of covered barges to do it in. So they selected 10 a.m., put 150 men into an open barge, gave them no breakfast, and left them in the barge two hours to move them 600 yards, and an hour unloading baggage afterwards! Result, out of my forty-nine, three heat-strokes on the spot, and four more sick the next day.

We left Basra on the 30th. It took us two-and-a-half days to do the 130 miles up here, against a strong wind and current. The Regiment has moved here from Nasiriyah. This place is 130 miles North of Basra and 120 South of Kut-el-Amarah (always known as Kut). As to our movements, the only kind of information I can give you would be something like this. There are fifteen thousand blanks, according to trustworthy reports, at blank. We have blank brigades and our troops are blanking at blank which is two-thirds of the way from here to blank; and I think our intention is to blank with all our three blanks as soon as possible, but this blank is remaining on lines of communications here for the present. Not very interesting is it? So I won't reel off any more.

From the little scraps of news that have come through, it looks as if the Balkans were going to be the centre of excitement. If Bulgaria has agreed to let the Germans through as I suspect she has, I'd bet on both Greece and Roumania joining the Allies.

Amarah.

September 4th, 1915.

To his Father.

We get hardly any news up here, so please kindly continue your function of war correspondent whenever you have time, and especially mention any casualties which affect me.

One of the few bits of news which have reached us is a report of a speech of yours in which you mention that Milner's Committee recommended the Government to guarantee 45s. a year for four years, but the Government wouldn't. Reuter deduces from this that we have found a way of keeping the whip hand of submarines: but it looks to me much more like Free Trade shibboleths + the fact that there has already been a 30% increase in the area under wheat. I hope you will have written me something about this.

Now for the military news. This battalion, when we arrived here, was nominally nearly 300 strong, but actually it could hardly have paraded 100. This reduction is nearly all due to sickness. The deaths from all causes only total between forty and fifty, out of the original 800: and of these about twenty-five, I think, were killed in action. But there has been an enormous amount of sickness during the hot weather, four-fifths of which has been heat-stroke and malaria. There have been a few cases of enteric and a certain number of dysentery; but next to heat and malaria more men have been knocked out by sores and boils than by any disease. It takes ages for the smallest sore to heal.

Of the original thirty officers, eight are left here, Major Stillwell, who is C.O., one Captain, Page-Roberts, a particularly nice fellow, and five subalterns, named Harris, Forbes, Burrell, Bucknill and Chitty: (Chitty is in hospital): and Jones, the M.O., also a very nice man and a pretty good M.O. too. The new Adjutant is a Captain from 2nd Norfolks named Floyd: he is also nice and seems good: was on Willingdon's staff and knows Jimmy.

In honour of our arrival, they have adopted Double Company system. I am posted to "A" Double Company, of which the Company Commander and only other officer is Harris, aet. 19. So I am second in command and four platoon commanders at once, besides having charge of the machine-guns (not that I am ever to parade with them) while Chitty is sick. It sounds a lot, but with next to no men about, the work is lessened. On paper, "A" D.C was seventy-two strong, which, with my fifty, makes 122: but in fact, of these 122, twenty-five are sick and sixteen detached permanently for duties at headquarters and so on, leaving eighty-one. And these eighty-one are being daily more and more absorbed into fatigues of various kinds and less and less available for parade. In a day or two we shall be the only English battalion remaining here, so that all the duties which can't be entrusted to Indian troops will fall on us.

I haven't had time to observe the birds here very much yet, but they seem interesting, especially the water-birds. With regard to what I wrote to Mamma about the teal, people who have been up the river say they saw a very big flock of them at Kut. There were a lot of snipe with them and about twenty bitterns, which surprises me. And about eighty miles north of here there is a mud flat where great numbers of mallards are assembling for migration northwards: and there are more bitterns there than there are higher up even. These flocks about the equinoxes are very curious. I expect the mallards will migrate northwards, and the teal soon afterwards will become very scarce, but I hope the bitterns will stay where they are. The snipe are less interesting: they move about all over the place, wherever they can pick up most food. These people put the size of the flock of teal at a hundred and fifty and the mallards at five hundred, but you should, I think, multiply the first by a hundred and the second only by ten.

I got Mamma's letter via the India Office just after we got here. I quite agree with her view of war, though I must admit the officers of 1/4 Hants seem to me improved by it. While sitting on that court martial at Agra I expressed my view in a sonnet which I append, for you to show to Mamma:

How long, O Lord, how long, before the flood Of crimson-welling carnage shall abate? From sodden plains in West and East the blood Of kindly men streams up in mists of hate Polluting Thy clear air: and nations great In reputation of the arts that bind The world with hopes of Heaven, sink to the state Of brute barbarians, whose ferocious mind Gloats o'er the bloody havoc of their kind, Not knowing love or mercy. Lord, how long Shall Satan in high places lead the blind To battle for the passions of the strong? Oh, touch thy children's hearts, that they may know Hate their most hateful, pride their deadliest foe.

I must stop now, as a mail is going out and one never knows when the next will be.

Norfolk House.

Amarah, *September 13th*, 1915.

To his Father.

As I have written the news to Mamma this week I will tell you what I gather of the campaign and country generally.

There's no doubt that old Townshend, the G.O.C., means to push on to Baghdad "ekdum"; and if the Foreign Office stops him there will be huge indignâ. It seems to me that the F.O. should have made itself quite explicit on the point, one way or the other months ago:

to pull up your general in full career is exasperating to him and very wasteful, as he has accumulated six months' supplies for an army of 16,000 up here, which will have to be mostly shipped back if he is pulled up at Kut. The soldiers all say the F.O. played the same trick on Barratt in the cold weather. They let him get to Qurnah, and he wanted and prepared to push on here and to Nasiryah, which were then the Turkish bases. But the F.O. stopped him and consequently the Turks could resume the offensive, and nearly beat us at Shaibah. The *political* people say that the soldiers had only themselves to thank they were nearly beaten at Shaibah. They were warned in December that the whole area between Sh. and Basrah would be flooded later on, and were urged either to dig a canal or build a causeway; but they pooh-poohed it: and consequently all supplies and ammunition at Shaibah had to be carried across 8 miles of marsh, 4ft. to 1in. deep.

As for the country, it is said to be very fertile wherever properly irrigated. At present the water is distributed about as badly as it could be. The annual rise of the river makes vast feverish swamps, and the rest of the country is waterless. Any stray Bedouin tribe that feels like growing a crop can go and cut a hole in the bank and irrigate a patch for one season and then leave it; and these cuts form new channels which as often as not lose themselves in a swamp. Meanwhile this haphazard draining off of the water is seriously impairing the main streams, especially that of the Euphrates, which is now almost unnavigable in the low water season. To develop the country therefore means (1) a comprehensive irrigation and drainage scheme. Willcock's scheme I believe is only for irrigation. I don't know how much the extreme flatness of the country would hamper such a scheme. Here we are 200 miles by river from the sea and only 28ft. above sea-level. It follows (2) that we must control the country and the nomad tribes from the highest *barrage* continuously down to the sea. (3) We must have security that the Turks don't interfere with the rivers above our barrage, or even neglect the river banks.

All this seems to me to point to a repetition of our Egyptian experience. We shall be drawn, whether we like it or not, into a virtual protectorate at least as far up as the line Kut-Nasiryah, along the Shatt-al-Hai, and that will have to extend laterally on the east to the Persian frontier and on the west to the Arabian tableland. I don't see how we can hope to get off with less: and that being so, I believe it would be better to take on the whole at once. North of the Shatt-al-Hai line (*i.e.* Kut-Nasiryah) it would be very exhausting to go, and very awkward politically, as you soon get among the holy places of the Shiahs, especially Karbala, which is their Mecca. But it's no use blinking the fact that a river is a continuous whole, and experience shows that the power which controls the mouth is sooner or later forced to climb to its source, especially when its up-stream neighbours are hostile and not civilised. And what power of Government will be left to Turkey after the war? It looks as if she will be as bankrupt, both financially and politically, as Persia; and I see no real hope of avoiding a partition à la Persia into British and Russian spheres of interest. In that case it seems to me the British sphere should go to the Shatt-al-Hai, and the Russian begin where the plain ends, or at any rate north of Mosul. Are you at liberty to tell me whether there is already an understanding with Russia about this country, and if so how far it goes?

As for the climate, I don't think it is any worse than the plains of India. When it is properly drained the fever will be much less: and under peace conditions the water can be properly purified and the heat dealt with. The obvious port is Basra; it is said that the bar outside Fao could easily be dredged to 26ft. The only other really good harbour is Koweit, I gather: but our game is to support the independence of K.: make it the railway terminus, but by using Basra you make your rail-freight as low as possible and have your commercial port where you can directly control matters.

I wish they would get a move on in the Dardanelles. It seems to me Germany is running a fearful risk by committing herself so deeply into the interior of Russia at this time of year. The only explanation I can find is that at each rush she has been much nearer to cutting off a Russian army than has transpired and so is tempted on: nearer perhaps than the Russians ever intended, which may be the reason of the Grand Duke's removal to the Caucasus.

Amarah.

September 11th.

To his Mother.

For the men, newspapers would be as welcome as anything. I think Papa might divert those weekly papers from Agra here, as they get a large supply in the Regimental Reading Room at Agra.

What strikes me about the 1/4th is that they are played out. They've no vitality left in them. Out of about 300 men there are seventy sick, mostly with trifling stomach or feverish attacks or sores, which a robust man would get over in two days; but it takes them a fortnight, and then a week or two afterwards they crock up again. One notices the same in their manner. They are listless and when off duty just lie about. When I see men bathing or larking it is generally some of our drafts. I hope the cold weather will brace them up a bit. I do wish I had more gifts in the entertaining line, though of course there are very few men left to entertain when you've allowed for all our guards and the men just off guard.

The house is two-storeyed, with thick brick walls, built round an open well-like court. There is a broad verandah all round the court, on to which every room opens. There is also a balcony on the W. side overlooking the river. We sleep on the roof a.p.u. The sun sets right opposite this balcony, behind a palm-grove, and the orange afterglows are reflected all up the westward bend of the river, which is very lovely: though personally I like the more thrilling cloud sunsets better than these still rich glowings of the desert.

The men sleep in huts just behind. These are sensibly built of brick. Only the S. side is walled up, and even there a space is left between the wall and the ceiling. The rest is just fenced with reed trellis work. The roofs are of reed matting, the floors brick with floor-boards for sleeping on. Boards and bedding are put out in the sun by day. The men are very contented in them. If I ask my men how they like it compared to India, they all say they like it better. "Why, you gets a decent dinner here, Sir." My experience quite confirms that of Sir Redvers Buller and other great authorities. If you feed T.A. well you can put him in slimy trenches and he'll be perfectly happy: but he'd never be contented in Buckingham Palace on Indian rations. Here we are of course on war rations, cheese, bacon and jam, bully beef and quite decent mutton, and condensed milk. Vegetables are scarce, so lime juice is an issue: and they are said just to have made beer one, which would be the crown of bliss. Every man gets (if he's there) five grains of quinine a day. There are, however, far fewer mosquitoes than I expected. I've only seen one myself. The only great pest is flies: but even of those there are far fewer here than in Basra.

When I hear what the 1/4th have been through, I think we are in luxury. They had a very rough trek to Ahway and Illah in Persia in May, and coming back much exhausted were stationed a month in Ashar Barracks (Basra). Here for a fortnight it never went below 100° by night and was 115° by day—damp heat:

and the barracks (Turkish) were in a state which precluded rest: the record bag for one man in one morning was sixty fleas from his puttees alone. And of course what Austen told the H. of C. about fans, ice and fruit was all eyewash.

A man in our Coy. died last night. I'd never seen him or knew he was ill. I was rather shocked at the way nobody seemed to care a bit. The Adjt. just looked in and said "who owns Pte. Taylor A." Harris said "I do: is he dead?" Adjt. "Yes: you must bury him to-morrow." Harris: "Right o." Exit Adjt. To do Harris justice, he doesn't know the man and thought he was still at Nasiriyah. None of the man's old Coy. officers are here.

Amarah.

September 21, 1915.

To his Mother.

The provision for the sick and wounded is on the whole fairly good now. Six months ago it was very inadequate, too few doctors and not enough hospital accommodation. My men who were in the Base Hospital at Basra spoke very well of it: it had 500 men in it then, and is capable of indefinite expansion. The serious cases are invalided to India by the hospital ship *Madras*. It is said that 10,000 have gone back to India in this way. It is a curious fact that the Indian troops suffered from heat-stroke every bit as much as the British.

There are now four hospitals here (1) a big one for native troops, (2) one for British troops which has expanded till it occupies three large houses, (3) one for British officers, which will be used for all ranks if the casualties next Saturday are heavy, (4) one for civilians. There seems to be no lack of drugs or dressings or invalid foods.

Amarah.

September 24, 1915.

To N.B.

Two letters from you rolled up together this mail, for both of which many thanks.

Like everyone else you write under the cloud of Warsaw and in the expectation of the enemy forthwith dashing back on us in the West. But the last two months have made it much harder for him to do that soon, if at all: and I hope the month which will pass before you get this will have made it harder still. I found it difficult weeks ago to explain what induced the Germans to commit themselves so deeply into the interior of Russia so late in the season, and I came to the conclusion that with each forward movement they had been much nearer to enveloping and smashing the Russians than the Reuters would have led one to suppose: and so had been lured on.

It now looks to me as if they are playing for one of two alternatives. If Von Below can get round their right flank he will try a last envelopment: if that flank falls back far enough to uncover Petrograd, he will make a dash for P. But all that will mean locking up even bigger forces in the East. Indeed it seems so reckless that I can only account for it by supposing either that they are confident of rushing Petrograd and paralysing Russia within a few weeks: or that they are in a desperate plight and know it.

As for the future, I think it would be a mistake to expect this war to produce a revolution in human nature and equally wrong to think nothing has been achieved if it doesn't. What I do hope is that it will mark a distinct stage towards a more Christian conception of international relations. I'm afraid that for a long time to come there will be those who will want to wage war and will have to be crushed with their own weapons. But I think this insane and devilish cult of war will be a thing of the past. War will only remain as an unpleasant means to an end. The next stage will be, one hopes, the gradual realisation that the ends for which one wages war are generally selfish: and anyway that law is preferable to force as a method of settling disputes. As to whether National ideals can be Christian ideals, in the strict sense they can't very well: because so large a part of the Christian ideal lies in self-suppression and self-denial which of course can only find its worth in individual conduct and its meaning in the belief that this life is but a preparation for a future life: whereas National life is a thing of this world and therefore the law of its being must be self-development and self-interest. The Prussians interpret this crudely as mere self-assertion and the will to power. The Christianising of international relations will be brought about by insisting on the contrary interpretation—that our highest self-development and interest is to be attained by respecting the interests and encouraging the development of others. The root fallacy to be eradicated of course, is that one Power's gain is another's loss; a fallacy which has dominated diplomacy and is the negation of law. I think we are perceptibly breaking away from it: the great obstacle to better thinking now is the existence of so many backward peoples incapable (as we think) of seeking their own salvation. Personally I don't see how we can expect the Christianising process to make decisive headway until the incapables are partitioned out among the capables. Meanwhile let us hope that each new war will be more unpopular and less respectable than the last.

I'm afraid I haven't even the excuse of a day's fishing without any fish.

Now for your letter of August 11th. I'm sorry you are discouraged because the programme you propounded to Auntie's work-party in February has not been followed. But comfort yourself with the reflection that the programme which Kaiser Bill propounded to *his* work-party has not been followed either.

Your Balkan programme, or rather Bob's, does not at present show much more sign of fulfilment than the one you propounded to Auntie's work-party, I'm afraid.

As usual nothing whatever has happened here. Elaborate arrangements have been made to have a battle to-morrow 120 miles up the river at Kut. It ought to be quite a big show: the biggest yet out here. As the floods are gone now it may be possible to walk right round them and capture the lot. If we pull off a big success the G.O.C. is very keen to push on to Baghdad, but it is a question whether the Cabinet will allow it. It means another 200 miles added to the L. of c.: and could only be risked if we were confident of the desert Arabs remaining quiet. Personally I see no solid argument for our going to Baghdad, and several against it (1) the advance would take us right through the sacred Shiah country, quite close to Karbala itself (Karbala is to the Shiah Mohammedans—and the vast majority of Indian Mahommedans are Shiahs—what Mecca is to the Sunnis; and Baghdad itself is a holy city). It would produce tremendous excitement in India and probably open mutiny among the Moslem troops here if they were ordered up. (2) Surely Russia wouldn't like it. (3) We can't expect to hold it permanently. Everything, so far as I can see, points to portioning this country into a British sphere and a Russian, with a neutral belt in between, on the Persian model, except that the "spheres" may be avowed protectorates. The British one must come up far enough to let us control the irrigation and drainage of Lower Mesopotamia properly: and stop short of the holy cities: say to the line Kut-el-Amarah (commonly called Kut)—Nasiriyah, along the Shatt-al-Hai. The Russians would, I suppose, come down to about Mosul.

This campaign is being conducted on gentlemanly lines. When we took a lot of prisoners at Nasiriyah we allowed the officers to send back for their kits. In return, last week, when one of our aeroplanes came down in the enemy's lines and the two airmen were captured, they sent a flag of truce across to us to let us know that the prisoners were unhurt and to fetch their kits.

I just missed Sir Mark Sykes who cruised through here two days ago. I have written to him in the hope of catching him on his way back.

Amarah.

September 27, 1915.

To R.K.

After censoring about 100 of my Company's letters I feel this will be a very incorrect performance. What strikes one too is the great gain in piquancy of style achieved by the omission of all punctuation. How could I equal this for instance "The Bible says this is a land of milk and honey there is plenty of water and dust about if thats what they mean?" or "The sentry shot an Arab one night soon after we got here I saw him soon afterwards caught him in the chest a treat it did."

I'm so glad to hear that Foss is getting on well: let me know the extent and nature of the damage. We hardly ever get a casualty list here: and I can't take that to mean there have been none lately: so my news of fractured friends hangs on the slender thread of the safe arrival of my *Times* every week—and on you and others who are not given to explaining that Bloggs will have given me all the news, no doubt.

The War Office, fond as ever of its little joke, having written my C.O. a solemn letter to say they couldn't entertain the idea of my promotion seeing that under the Double Coy. system the establishment of Captains is reduced to seven and so on, and having thereby induced him to offer me the unique felicity of bringing a draft to this merry land, has promptly gazetted my promotion, and antedated it to April 2nd, so that I find myself a Double Coy. Commander and no end of a blood. My importance looks more substantial on paper than on parade: for of the 258 men in "A" Double Coy. I can never muster more than about thirty in the flesh. You see so many have overeaten themselves on the ice and fresh vegetables which Austen dwelt upon in the H. of C. or have caught chills from the supply of punkahs and fans (*ib.*) that 137 have been invalided to India and twenty-five more are sick here. Then over fifty are on jobs which take them away from the Coy. and from ten to twenty go on guards every day. However my dignity is recognised by the grant of a horse and horse allowance.

Unless it is postponed again, the great battle up-river should be coming off to-day. I hope it is, as it is the coolest day we've had since April. In fact it is a red-letter day, being the first on which the temperature has failed to reach 100° in this room. You wouldn't believe me how refreshing a degree 96° can be.

We have also heard fairy-tale like rumours of an advance of Four Thousand Yards in France, but I have not seen it in black and white yet.

Having so few men available there are not many parades, in fact from 7 to 8 a.m. about four times a week is all that I've been putting in. And as a tactful Turk sank the barge containing all my Company's documents sometime in July there is an agreeable shortage of office business. So I am left to pass a day of cultured leisure and to meditate on the felicity of the Tennysonian "infinite torment of flies." I read Gibbon and Tennyson and George Eliot and the *Times* by turns, with intervals of an entertaining work, the opening sentence of which is

"Birds are warm-blooded vertebrate animals oviparous and covered with feathers, the anterior limbs modified into wings, the skull articulating with the vertebral column by a single occipital condyle" and so on. I also work spasmodically at Hindustani. I rather fancy my handwriting in the Perso-Arabic script. Arabic proper I am discouraged from by the perverse economy of its grammar and syntax. It needs must have two plurals, one for under ten and one for over, twenty-three conjugations, and yet be without the distinction of past and future. Which is worse even than the Hindustani alphabet with no vowels and four z's—so *unnecessary*, isn't it, as my Aunts would say.

Amarah.

September 29, 1915.

To his Father.

One's system has got so acclimatised to high temperatures that I find it chilly and want my greatcoat to sit in at any temperature under 80°, under 100° is noticeably warm.

The men are getting livelier already and the sick list will soon, I hope, shrink. The chief troubles are dust and flies. About four days per week a strong and often violent wind blows from the N.W., full of dust from the desert, and this pervades everything. The moment the wind stops the flies pester one. They all say that this place is flyless compared to Nasiriyah, where they used to kill a pint and a half a day by putting saucers of formalin and milk on the mess table and still have to use one hand with a fan all the time while eating with the other, to prevent getting them into their mouths. Here it is only a matter of half a dozen round one's plate—we feed on the first floor, which is a gain. In the men's bungalows I try to keep them down by insisting on every scrap of food being either swept away or covered up: and the presence or absence of flies is incidentally a good test as to whether the tables and mugs, etc., have been properly cleaned. They are worse in the early morning. When I ride through the town before breakfast they settle all up the sunny side of me from boot to topi, about two to the square inch, and nothing but hitting them will make them budge. They are disgusting creatures. Of course the filthy habits of the natives encourage them. The streets are littered with every kind of food-scraps and dirt: and the Arab has only two W.C.'s—the street and the river. Our chief tyranny in his eyes is that we have posted sanitary police about who fine him 2s. if he uses either:

but like all reforms it is evaded on a large scale. The theory that the sun sweetens everything is not quite true. Even after several days' sun manure is very offensive and prolific: and many parts of the streets are not reached by the sun at all: and in any case the flies get to work much sooner than the sun.

We have just had news from the front that a successful action has been fought, the enemy's left flank turned and several hundred prisoners taken—our own casualties under 500. So the show seems to have come off up to time. We were afraid it might have to be postponed, as a raiding party got round and cut our L. of C., but this does not appear to have worried them. I hope they will be able to follow this success up and capture all their guns and stores, if not a large proportion of their forces.

Two days ago we got the best news that we have had for a very long time from both European fronts, an advance of from one to three miles over nearly half the Western front, with about 14,000 prisoners: and Russian reports of 8,000 dead in front of one position and captures totalling something like 20,000. Since then no news has come through, which is very tantalising, as one longs to know whether the forward move has been continued. I am afraid even if it has there will be more enormous casualty lists than ever.

The most boring thing about this place is that there are no amusing ways of taking exercise, which is necessary to keep one fit. As a double Coy. Commander I have a horse, a quiet old mare which does nothing worse than shy and give an occasional little buck on starting to canter. But the rides are very dull. There are only three which one may call A, B and C, thus:

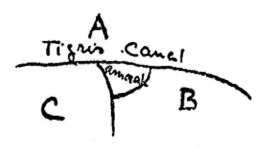

A is the flooded area, and when it is dry it is caked as hard as brick, and not a vegetable to vary the landscape.

B takes one through the little ground, the four cemeteries, and the deserted brick-kilns: by the time one is through these it is generally time to go home: and even beyond it is market gardens and one can only ride on foot-paths: and there are only two foot-paths through the barbed wire defences.

C is good soft-surfaced desert, much the best riding ground though its virtues are negative. But to reach it one has to cross the Tigris by the boat-bridge, and this is apt to be cut at any moment for the passage of boats, which means a delay of half an hour, not to be lightly risked before breakfast: and in the afternoons the interval between excessive sun and darkness is very brief. It is too hot to ride with pleasure before 4.30 and the sun sets at 5.30: and the dusty wind is at its worst till about 5.

Amarah.

October 7, 1915.

To his Brother.

Thanks awfully for your letter. It was one of the best I've had for a long time. And many congratulations on the birth of a daughter. I'm delighted it went off so well, and only hope she and Grace are both flourishing.

I am sorry to hear about Benison. I suppose he was in some unit or other. You saw of course that Stolley was killed some time ago.

At present, at any rate, we're a very comfortable distance behind the firing line. This has been the advanced base for the Kut show. By river we are 130 miles above Basra and about the same below Kut. The action there on the 27th and 28th was a great success, but the pursuit was unfortunately hung up and prevented our reaping quite the full fruits. This was partly due to a raid on our L. of C. scuppering some barge-loads of fuel, but chiefly to the boats getting stuck on mud banks. This river is devilish hard to navigate just now. It winds like a corkscrew, and though it looks 150 yards wide, the navigable channel is quite narrow, and only 4ft. to 6ft. deep at that. So all the river boats have to be flat bottomed, and the strong current and violent N.W. wind keeps pushing them on the mud banks at every bend.

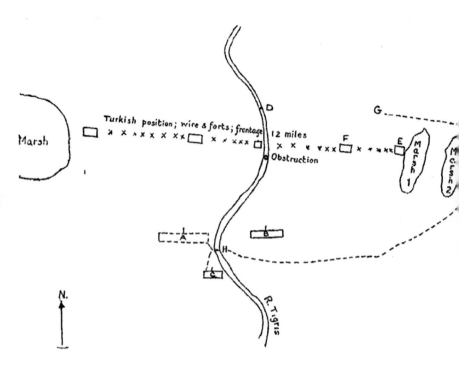

The Turks had, they think, 15,000 men and 32 guns. Their position was twelve miles long and most elaborately entrenched and wired with all the German devices, and rested on a marsh at either end.

We had about 10,000 men of all arms and 25 or 27 guns, seven of them on river boats, I think. Townshend's attack was as follows. He made all his reconnaissances and preparations as for an attack on their right flank, and on Monday, 27th he deployed a brigade, A. on that side of the river, leaving only two battalions, B. on the right bank, and keeping two battalions in reserve, C. For various reasons this attack had made very little progress by sunset and was last seen digging itself in. Then as soon as it got dark almost the whole of A. together with the reserve C. was ordered to march round to the enemy's left flank and attack Fort E. at dawn. So they moved off, intending to go between Marsh 1 and Marsh 2; but in the dark they went round outside Marsh 2, and at dawn after a twelve mile march found themselves at G. They completely surprised and quickly captured Fort E. and the section E. and F., their casualties here being mainly from our own artillery, as was inevitable: but they were enfiladed from F. and had to reform and dig themselves in on a front parallel with the river, and send for artillery support.

Meanwhile the skeleton left on our left flank and the force B. were pressing a frontal attack, supported by the guns: and by the afternoon the outflanking force A. was able to resume its advance, which it was keen to finish as the men were very tired and had run out of water. But just then the whole Turkish reserve turned up on their right front and flank, having been hurried back from the right flank to which our feint had drawn them, across the bridge D. whence they deployed in crescent formation. Apparently this new danger had a very bracing effect on the thirsty ones; it is a rash man that stands between T.A. and his drink. They went straight for the centre of the crescent, as far as I can make out, with the Turkish reserves on their front and flanks and the Turkish firing line in their rear. This was where most of the casualties occurred, but after a stiff fight the Turks broke and ran: and there was a tremendous crush at the bridge D. where they started shooting each other freely.

Meanwhile, the Turkish Commander announced that he had received a telegram from the Sultan requiring the immediate presence of himself and army at Constantinople: so the firing line took the hint and started for the new alignment by the shortest route. However, as everybody's great idea was to put the river between himself and the enemy he'd been facing, two streams met at the bridge D. and there were further scenes. By this time it was dark, and our troops were utterly exhausted, so nothing more was done for the moment.

Our casualties were 85 killed and 1,158 wounded, an extraordinary proportion. We haven't had any reliable information of the enemy's losses yet: but we took about 1,300 prisoners.

I must stop now. I am very fit and a Capt., 3rd Senior Officer out here for the moment (excluding Adjutant O.M.O.) and am commanding "A" double Coy.

Amarah.

October 8, 1915

To N.B.

Two lots of letters arrived this mail, including yours of August 30th and September 6th, for which many thanks.

If I said that this war means the denying of Christianity I ought to have explained myself more. That phrase is so often used loosely that people don't stop to think exactly what they mean. If the Germans deliberately brought about the war to aggrandise themselves, as I believe they did, that was a denial of Christianity, *i.e.* a deliberate rejection of Christian principles and disobedience to Christ's teaching: and it makes no difference in that case that it was a national and not an individual act. But once the initiating evil was done, it involved the consequence, as evil always does, of leaving other nations only a choice of evils. In this case the choice for England was between seeing Belgium and France crushed, and war. In choosing war I can't admit there was any denial of Christianity, and I don't think you can point to any text, however literally you press the interpretation, which will bear a contrary construction. Take "Resist not him that doeth evil" as literally as you like, in its context. It obviously refers to an individual resisting a wrong committed against himself, and the moral basis of the doctrine seems to me twofold: (1) As regards yourself, self-denial, loving your enemies, etc., is the divine law for the soul; (2) as regards the wronger nothing is so likely to better him as your unselfish behaviour. The doctrine plainly does not refer to wrongs committed in your presence against others. Our Lord Himself overthrew the tables of the money-changers. And the moral basis of His resistance to evil here is equally clear if you tolerate evils committed against others: (1) your own morale and courage is lowered: it is shirking; (2) the wronger is merely encouraged. If I take A.'s coat and A. gives me his cloak also, I may be touched. But B.'s acquiescence in the proceeding cannot possibly touch me and only encourages me. Now the Government of a country is nearly always in the position of B. not A., because a country is not an individual. In our case we were emphatically in the position of B.: but I would justify the resistance of Belgium on the same grounds.

Of course as I said last week, national standards can't be as self-sacrificing as individual standards: and never can be until all the individuals in a nation are so Christian as to choose unanimously the self-sacrificing course.

I agree that the Dardanelles outlook is very serious, and it now looks as if Germany had got Bulgaria to come in against us. We ought to concentrate on a decision there as vigorously as the Germans did in Poland, and let us hope with more success.

The big offensive in France came off and seems to have done remarkably well for a few days: but we have heard nothing more of it for over a week. I'm afraid that means we exhausted ourselves and lost heavily.

The outstanding fact here is that the hot weather is over. It is now only unpleasant to be out from 10 till 4, and then only in the sun. The transition is going on rapidly and by the end of this month I expect to see cold weather conditions established. I have played football twice and been out shooting twice. There is a large black partridge to be shot here which is very good to eat.

I can give you no details about the Kut fight. In fact you probably know more than we do: I must stop now.

Amarah.

October 11, 1915.

To L.R.

The weather has got cooler so rapidly that I have been shooting and playing football quite happily. The chief things to shoot are a big black partridge (which will soon be extinct) and a little brown dove, later on there are snipe, and already there are duck, but these are unapproachable. Many thanks for your letters of August 27th, and September 8th, which arrived together this mail.

I think Mrs. Ricketts takes an unduly optimistic view when she says the Germans mean the war to be decided out here. Nothing would suit us better. Meanwhile, we certainly seem to mean to go to Baghdad, and that will mean at least one other big fight: but so far they show no sign of moving us up to the firing line. This last show was a big success and nearly was a much bigger, only our men having fought for two days and marched twelve miles in the intervening night and having run out of water, were not able to press the pursuit very vigorously. I take it the next show will come off in about three weeks' time, sooner if possible.

I have heard a good deal vaguely about the Angels at Mons. It is very interesting. I gather that A. Machen wrote a magazine story and that this has got embodied with the real stories and is therefore supposed to have originated them. If Begbie's forthcoming book on them is good, do send it to me. We have had no such stories out here, so far as I know.

As to being pessimistic about the future, I think our mistake was to underestimate Germany's striking force. You must always keep the German calculations in mind as well as our hopes, and you will see that the former have been falsified quite as much as the latter—in fact much more. They calculated—and not without having worked it all out thoroughly—that their superior armaments and mobility would enable them (1) to smash France within a few weeks, (2) to manœuvre round the Russians and defeat their armies in detail till they sued for peace, (3) to dominate the continent and organise it for the settlement with England. We ought to be devoutly thankful that (1) failed: but Instead we assumed that the worst was over and that (2) would fail as signally. As a matter of fact (2) looks like failing after all; but it has been near success for much longer than (1) was and consequently has achieved more. But if you remember, both Papa and K. said at the outset it would be a three years' war: which clearly meant that they expected us to get the worst of it the first year, equalise matters the second year and not be decisively victorious till the third year.

Luly has plenty of friends at Agra and is really very happy there, so you may be at ease about him.

Many thanks for your offer to send us things for the cold. But the danger is overlapping, so I will refer you to Mamma, to whom I wrote about it some time back: and I hope *she* is combining with Mrs. Bowker of Winchester (wife of 1/4th Colonel) who is organising the sending of things to the battalion as a whole. You might mention to Mamma that, in addition to the articles I've told her of, newspapers and magazines would be very acceptable.

Amarah.

October 17, 1915.

To N.B.

Many thanks for your little letter wishing me Godspeed out here, it has only just followed me on, and reached me soon after your letter of September 12th in which you ask me about Persia. I assure you I know less of what is happening in Persia—though we can see the Persian hills from here—than you do. Your letter was my first news of the Consul General's death, which I have seen since in *The Times* as well. All I know is that German gold working on the chronic lawlessness has made the whole country intolerably disturbed. The Government is powerless. The disorder is mainly miscellaneous robbery: in the north there is a good deal of hostility to Russia, but nothing approaching organised war or a national rising. In May Arab raiders threatened Ahwaz where the Anglo-Persian Oil Company's pipe-line runs; and at the Persian Government's request a force, including 1/4 Hants, went up there and dispersed them. Then in August the unrest in Bushire got acute, and two officers were killed in an ambush. So they sent a force to occupy it. I don't know how large it was; I imagine two battalions or so and a few guns. Since then I've heard nothing. Mark Sykes, whom I saw about October 6th, said he thought things were quieter there now.

For the Persian situation generally, up to last year, the best account I've seen is in Gilbert Murray's pamphlet on "The Foreign Policy of Sir E. Grey." There's no doubt these weak corrupt semi-civilised States are a standing temptation to intriguers like the Germans and so a standing danger to peace. That is going to be the crux here too, after the war. If I make up my mind and have the energy, I will write my views more fully on the subject in a week or two.

There is a lull here and no news. But there seems no doubt that we are going to push up to Baghdad. The enemy are now in their last and strongest position, only twenty miles from B.: and we are concentrating against it. Undoubtedly large reinforcements are on their way up, but we don't know how many. I expect you may look for news from these parts about November 7th.

It is getting quite cold. Yesterday the wind began again and we all had to take to our overcoats, which seems absurd as it was over 80°. To-day it was only 74° indoors all the morning and we sat about in "British warms." And the nights seem Arctic. To get warm last night I had to get into my flea-bag and pile a sheet, a rug and a kaross on top of that: it was 70° when I went to bed and went down to 62° at dawn. As it goes down to 32° later on, I foresee we shall be smothered in the piles of bed-clothes we shall have to accumulate.

I continue to play football and ride intermittently. I believe I could mount a middle-sized English horse without serious inconvenience now. I have begun to try to pick up a little Arabic from the functionary known as the Interpreter.

Amarah.

October 18, 1915.

To M.H.

I'm so glad the saris are what you wanted. If you pay £5 into my a/c at Childs, it will be simplest.

Everyone—except I suppose the victims—seems to have regarded the Zeppelin raid as a first-class entertainment. I think they do us vastly more good than harm, but it would be a satisfaction to bag one.

So poor Charles Lister was killed after all. He is a tremendous loss. And ——, who could have been spared much better, has been under fire in Gallipoli for months without being touched.

I agree with Charlie's sentiments. What is so desperately trying about the Army system is that mere efflux of time puts a man who may be, and generally is, grossly stupid, in command of much more intelligent people, whose lives are at his bungling mercy. If Napoleon, who won his Italian campaign at 27, had been in the British Army he wouldn't have become a Major till 1811. It is an insane system which no business would dream of adopting. Yet it wouldn't do to abolish it, or you destroy the careers of 4/5 of your Officers. The reform I should like would be to make every third promotion in any regiment compulsorily regardless of seniority.

I am having a few lessons in Arabic now, but it is a much more difficult language than Hindustani, and the only available "Munshi" is the regimental interpreter who can't read and speaks very broken English, and the only available book deals with classical Egyptian and Syrian Arabic, which are to the Arabic of to-day as Latin, French and Italian are to Spanish. So my acquirements are likely to be limited.

There is absolutely no news here. Reinforcements are said to be coming but have not arrived. The next show should come off about November 10th.

Amarah.

October 11, 1915.

To R.K.

I have just seen in the *Times* that Charles Lister died of his wounds. It really is heart-breaking. All the men one had so fondly hoped would make the world a little better to live in seem to be taken away. And Charles was a spirit which no country can afford to lose. I feel so sorry for you too: he must have been very dear to you personally. How the world will hate war when it can pause to think about it.

I had quite a cheerful letter from Foss this mail. I wonder he wasn't more damaged, as the bullet seems to have passed through some very important parts of him. I am rather dreading the lists which are bound to follow on our much-vaunted advance of three weeks ago. As for the Dardanelles, it is an awful tragedy. And now with

Bulgaria against us and Greece obstructed by her King, success is farther off than ever.

No, Luly is not with me: I was the only officer with the draft. As for impressions of our surroundings they are definite but not always communicable.

If this neighbourhood could certainly be identified with Eden, one could supply an entirely new theory of the Fall of Adam. Here at Amarah we are 200 miles by river from the sea and 28ft. above sea level. Within reach of the water anything will grow: but as the Turks levied a tax on trees the date is the only one which has survived. There are little patches of corn and fodder-stuff along the banks, and a few vegetable gardens round the town. Otherwise the whole place is a desert and as flat as this paper: except that we can see the bare brown Persian mountains about forty miles off to the N.N.E.

The desert grows little tufts of prickly scrub here and there, otherwise it is like a brick floor. In the spring it is flooded, and as the flood recedes the mud cakes into a hard crust on which a horse's hoof makes no impression; but naturally the surface is very rough in detail, like a muddy lane after a frost. So it is vile for either walking or riding.

The atmosphere can find no mean between absolute stillness—which till lately meant stifling heat—and violent commotion in the form of N.W. gales which blow periodically, fogging the air with dust and making life almost intolerable while they last. These gales have ceased to be baking hot, and in another month or two they will be piercingly cold.

The inhabitants are divided into Bedouins and town-Arabs. The former are nomadic and naked, and live in hut-tents of reed matting. The latter are just like the illustrations in family Bibles.

What I *should* be grateful for in the way of literature is if you could find a portable and readable book on the history of these parts. I know it's rather extensive, but if there are any such books on the more interesting periods you might tell Blackwell to send them to me: I've got an account there. My Gibbon sketches the doings of the first four Caliphs: but what I should like most would be the subsequent history, the Baghdad Caliphs, Tartar Invasion, Turkish Conquest, etc. For the earlier epochs something not too erudite and very popular would be most suitable. Mark Sykes tells me he is about to publish a Little Absul's History of Islam, but as he is still diplomatising out here I doubt if it will be ready for press soon.

As for this campaign, you will probably know more about the Kut battle than I do. Anyway the facts were briefly these. The Turks had a very strongly entrenched position at Kut, with 15,000 men and 35 guns. We feinted at their right and then outflanked their left by a night march of twelve miles. (Two brigades did this, while one brigade held them in front.) Then followed a day's hard fighting as the out-flankers had to storm three redoubts successfully before they could properly enfilade the position. Just as they had done it the whole Turkish reserve turned up on their right and they had to turn on it and defeat it, which they did. But by that time it was dark, the troops were absolutely exhausted and had finished all their water. Nobody could tell how far the river was, so the only thing to do was to bivouac and wait for daylight. In the night the Turks cleared out and got away. If we could have pressed on and seized their bridge, we should have almost wiped them out: but it was really wonderful we did as much as we did under the circumstances. Our casualties were 1243, but only 85 killed. The Turkish losses are not known: we captured about 1400 and 12 of the guns: we buried over 400, but don't know how many the local Arabs buried. Our pursuit was delayed by the mud-banks on the river, and the enemy was able to get clear and reform in their next position, about ninety miles further north. We are now concentrating against them and it is authoritatively reported that large reinforcements have been sent from India. This means they intend going for Baghdad. It seems to me rash: but I suppose there is great need to assert our prestige with the Moslem world, even at the expense of our popularity: for B. is a fearfully sacred place.

I should also like from Blackwell's a good and up-to-date map of these parts, *i.e.* from the Troad to the Persian Gulf.

Amarah.

October 21, 1915.

To his Mother.

It is hard from here to be patient with the Government for not taking a bolder line all round and saying frankly what they want. They are omnipotent if they would only lead. Now we hear that Carson has resigned. I can't hitch that on to the conscription crisis, yet it doesn't say it is from ill-health: it is a puzzle.

Life is as uneventful as usual here. I have nearly finished *The Woman in White*. It is really one of the best thrillers I've read, and Count Fosco more than fulfils my expectations: I wonder if Haldane keeps white mice. I have also finished Tennyson. I have read him right through in the course of the year, which is much the best way to read a poet, as you can follow the development of his thoughts. His mind, to my thinking, was profound but not of very wide range, and strangely abstract. His only pressing intellectual problems are those of immortality and evil, and he reached his point of view on those before he was forty. He never advances or recedes from the position summarised in the preface to "In Memoriam," d. 1849. The result is that his later work lacks the inspiration of restlessness and discovery, and he tends to put more and more of his genius into the technique of his verse and less into the meaning. The versification is marvellous, but one gets tired of it, and he often has nothing to say and has to spin out commonplaces in rich language. One feels this even in the "Idylls of the King," which are the best of his later or middle long efforts: they are artificial, not impulsive; Virgil, not Homer; Meredith calls them 'dandiacal flutings,' which is an exaggeration. But I can quite see how irritating Tennyson must be to ardent sceptics like Meredith and the school which is now in the ascendant. To them a poet is essentially a rebel, and Tennyson refused to be a rebel. That is why they can't be fair to him and accuse him of being superficial. I think that a very shallow criticism of him. He saw and states the whole rebels' position—"In Memoriam" is largely a debate between the Shelley-Swinburne point of view and the Christian. Only he states it so abstractly that to people familiar with Browning's concrete and humanised dialectic it seems cold and artificial. But it's really his sincerest and deepest thought, and he deliberately rejects the rebel position as intellectually and morally untenable: and adopts a position of aquiescent agnosticism on the problem of evil subject to an unshakeable faith in immortality and the Love of God. This is a red rag to your Swinburnes. That is why I asked you to send me Swinburne, as I want to get to the bottom of his position. Shelley's I know, and it is, in my opinion a much more obvious, easier, and more superficial one than Tennyson's: besides being based on a distorted view of Christianity. Shelley in fact wanted to abolish Christianity as the first step towards teaching men to be Christian.

Of all the agnostics, Meredith is the one that appeals to me most: but I've not read his poetry, which I believe has much more of his philosophy in it than his novels have.

P.S. I have just seen your appeal in the *Hampshire Herald* for £500 for a motor ambulance boat, in which you say the Red Cross have already sent us two such boats. All I can say is that nobody in this regiment has ever seen or heard of these boats: and they certainly have not been used for transporting sick and wounded either from Nasiriyah or from Kut. If they were in Mesopotamia at all, it is incredible that we shouldn't have heard of them.

Amarah.

October 22, 1915.

To L.R.

I don't think there is any likelihood of Luly's coming here. For one thing our battalion 1/6th is too weak to afford another draft at present; and even if it sent one there are many officers who would be asked before Luly. As a matter of fact we have just heard we 1/4th are getting large reinforcements from our proper resources, *viz.* 250 from 2/4th at Quetta and 50 from those invalided in the hot weather.

Your letter of September 5th arrived well after that of September 22nd.

I'm glad the —— are optimistic: if Belgians can be we should be able to. But I can't help feeling the Government is lamentably weak and wanting in leadership: the policy of keeping the nation in the dark seems to me to be insane.

There is no news to report here. We still do very little work, but the weather is quite pleasant. I am very well.

There is not much to do. The country is very dull for walking and riding.

The birds here are very few compared to those in India. On the river there are pied Kingfishers. On the flooded land and especially on the mud-flats round it there are large numbers of sandpipers, Kentish and ringed plovers, stints and stilts, terns and gulls, ducks and teal, egrets and cranes: but as there is not a blade of vegetation within a mile of them there are no facilities for observation, still less for shooting.

There are several buzzards and falcons and a few kites, but vultures are conspicuous by their absence. There are no snakes or crocodiles either. Scavenging is left to dogs and jackals; and there is a hooded crow, not very abundant, which is peculiar to this country, having white where the European and Eastern Asiatic species have grey—a handsome bird. In the river there are a few sharks and a great abundance of a carp-like fish which runs up to a very large size. The Quartermaster can buy two 70lb. fish every morning for the men's breakfasts, and has been offered one of 120lb.

Amarah,

October 31, 1915.

To N.B.

I do hope your "fifty submarines" is true. I shan't think much of you if you can't get official confirmation from Cousin Arthur: but if he is impenetrably discreet, you might at least get him to explain—or pass it on to me if you know already—what conceivable harm it could do if we published the bare numbers of submarines "accounted for" without any particulars of when, where, or how.

As for this campaign it is the old story of the Empire repeating itself. When it began they only meant to secure the oil-pipe and protect British interests at Basra. But they found to their great surprise that you can't stay comfortably on the lower waters of a great river with an enemy above you any more than you could live in a flat with the lodger above continually threatening your life. A river like the Tigris or Euphrates is a unit, and the power which occupies its mouth will inevitably be drawn to its source unless it meets the boundaries of a strong and civilised state on the way. Turkey will be neither after the war.

What has happened so far?

Dec.-Jan.

We occupied the Shattal-Arab as far as Kurnah. We sat still. The Turks, based on Nasiriyah attacked us and nearly recaptured Basra.

April

We beat them at Shaiba, and for safety's sake had to push them from their base.

May

Then the double advance to Amarah and Nasiriyah.

July

We pushed the Turks out, and they promptly reformed at Kut and prepared to threaten us again. So we pushed forward again and beat them at Kut.

September

Now they have reformed at a point, only twenty miles from ——, their present base. We shall go for them there no doubt, and push them back once more. But what does it all lead to? Imagine peace restored. What will Turkey be like? She will be bankrupt, chaotic, totally incapable of keeping order among these murderous Bedouins. The country would be a second Persia under her. Persia is intolerable enough for the Europeans who trade there at present: but the plight of this country might easily be worse. We are bound to control the bit from Basra to the sea to protect existing interests. The whole future of that area—as of all Mesopotamia—depends on a scientific scheme of drainage and irrigation. At present half the country is marsh and half desert. Why? Because under Turkish rule the river is never dredged, the banks are never repaired, stray Arabs can cut haphazard canals and leave them to form marshes, and so on. Now an irrigation and drainage scheme is vitally necessary, but (1) it involves a large outlay; (2) to be effective it must start a long way up-stream; (3) there must be security for the good government *not only* of the area included in the scheme, but of the whole course of the river above it. These Asiatic rivers are tricky things: they run for hundreds of miles through alluvial plains which are as flat as your hand. Here at Amarah, 200 miles from the mouth of the Tigris, we are only 28ft. above sea-level. Consequently the river's course is very easily altered. Look at Stanford's map of this region and see how the Euphrates has lost itself between Nasiriyah and Basra—"old channel," "new channel," creeks, marshes, lakes, flood-areas and so on; the place is a nightmare. That kind of thing is liable to happen anywhere if the river is neglected. So that our schemes for Lower Mesopotamia might be spoilt by the indolence of those in possession higher up the river: let alone the security of the trade-routes which would be at the mercy of wild Arabs if Turkey collapses.

All this inclines me more and more to believe that we shall be forced, sooner or later, to occupy the whole Mesopotamian plain as far as Mosul or to whatever point is the southern limit of Russian control. At first I favoured a "neutral zone" from Mosul to Kut, and I shouldn't be surprised if that plan still finds favour at home. But frankly I see no prospect of a strong enough Government to make the neutral zone workable; on the contrary everything points to the absorption of the Persian neutral zone by either us or Russia, probably us.

I am still a Captain, but no longer a Coy. Commander. A large draft from India has arrived, 11 officers and 319 men from 1/4th and 2/4th, invalids returned. I am now second in command of a Coy. of respectable size.

Amarah.

October 10, 1915.

To his Father.

I agree with most of your reflections about the moral justification of war. War is an evil, because it is the product of sin and involves more sin and much suffering. But that does not mean it is necessarily wrong to fight. Once evil is at work, one of its chief results is to leave good people only a choice of evils, wherein the lesser evil becomes a duty. I'm not prepared to say we've been wholly guiltless in the whole series of events which produced this war: but in the situation of July, 1914, produced as it was by various sinful acts, I am quite sure it was our duty to fight, and that it is our duty to fight on till German militarism is crushed. And I certainly can't believe we ought not to have made such a treaty with Belgium as we did. You've got to face the fact that the spirit which produces war is still dominant. Fight that spirit by all means: but while it exists don't suppose your own duty is merely to keep out of wars. That seems to me a very selfish and narrow view. As for our Lord in a bayonet charge, one doesn't easily imagine it: but that is because it is inconsistent with His mission, rather than His character. I can't imagine a Christian *enjoying* either a bayonet charge, or hanging a criminal, or overthrowing the tables of a money-changer, or any other form of violent retribution.

Your sight of the Zeppelin must have been thrilling. You don't make it clear whether it was by day or night. I am curious to see if my next batch of *Times* will mention it. Clearly it is very hard to damage Zs. by gun-fire: but I don't understand quite why our aeroplanes can't do more against them. Do they get right back to Germany before daylight?

I have been out shooting three times this week, with Patmore of 1/7th Hants, and we got three partridges, six partridges and seven doves respectively. The partridges are big black ones, as large as young grouse, and very good to eat: but they will soon be extinct here as we are operating much in the same way as "the officers" do at Blackmoor. The doves were reported as sand-grouse, and certainly come flighting in from the desert very much in the s.-g. manner: but they are very like turtle doves when shot.

On our way home after the first shoot, I saw a falcon catch a swallow on the wing. It had missed one and we were watching it. It flew straight and rather fast past us, just within shot, fairly high. A swallow came sailing at full speed from the opposite direction and would have passed above and to the right of the falcon, and about 6ft. from it. The latter took no notice of it till the crucial moment, when it swerved and darted upwards, exactly as a swallow itself does after flies, and caught the swallow neatly in its talons. It then proceeded on its way so calmly that if you had taken your eye off it for 1/5th second you wouldn't have known it had deviated from its course. It then planed down and settled about 400 yards away on the ground.

I have written to Top such details of the Kut battle as I could gather from eye-witness: but I don't think it forms a reliable account, and you will probably find the official version rather different, when it comes out. Anyway it appears to be beyond doubt now that we mean to push on to Baghdad, in spite of your *Beatus possidens*. It was only lack of water and the exhaustion of the troops which prevented a much larger haul this time: and now they are concentrating against the next position, 90 miles further north. We hear again on good authority that 8,000 reinforcements are coming out. They will certainly be needed if we are to hold Baghdad. It seems to me a very rash adventure: especially as Bulgaria's intervention may enable the Turks to send an Army Corps down to Baghdad, in which case we should certainly have to retire.

Amarah.

All Saints, 1915.

To R.K.

Your letters have been so splendidly regular that I'm afraid a gap of three weeks may mean you've been ill: but

I can't be surprised at anyone at home breaking down under the constant strain of nearness and frequent news. Mesopotamia and a bi-weekly Reuter are certainly efficient sedatives; and the most harrowing crisis of the Russian armies is only rescued from the commonplace by its unintelligibility. Even the heart-breaking casualties, reaching us five weeks old, have nothing like the stab they have in England.

Life here requires a Jane Austen to record it. Our interests are focussed on the most ridiculous subjects. Recently they took an ecclesiastical turn, which I think should be reported to you. The station was left "spiritually" in charge of a Y.M.C.A. deacon for a fortnight: and discussion waxed hot in the Mess as to what a Deacon was. The prevailing opinion was that he "was in the Church," but not "consecrated"; so far Lay instinct was sound, if a little vague. Then our Scotch Quartermaster laid it down that a Deacon was as good as a Parson in that he could wear a surplice, but inferior to a parson in that he couldn't marry you. But the crux which had most practical interest for us was whether he could bury us. It was finally decided that he could: but fortunately in actual fact his functions were confined to organising a football tournament and exhibiting a cinema film.

He was succeeded by a priest from the notorious diocese of Bombay: who proceeded to shift the table which does duty for altar to the E. side of the R.A.T.A. room and furnish the neighbourhood of it into a faint resemblance to a Church. But what has roused most speculation is the "green thing he wears over his surplice for the early service and takes off before Parade service." I suggested that it was a precaution against these chilly mornings.

Gibbon has more to say about these parts than I thought: and I find he alludes to them off and on right down to 1453, so if you haven't been able to find a suitable book, I can carry on with that philosopher's epitome.

A large draft has just reached us from India, 11 officers and 319 men. They are partly returned invalids, but mainly 2/4th from Quetta. We shall now be a fairly respectable strength.

Cold weather conditions are almost established now. It is only over 80° for a few hours each day, and between 8 p.m. and 9 a.m. I wear a greatcoat. A senior captain having arrived with the draft has taken over "A" Coy. and I remain as second in command. There is singularly little to do at present—about one hour per day.

I wonder if you know any of the officers in this push. There is Chitty of Balliol, a contemporary of Luly's: and one Elton among the newly-joined, said to be a double first.

They have made me censor of civil telegrams.

I see no prospect of peace for a year yet, and not much of our leaving this country till well after peace. I used to think I wasn't easily bored: but it is hard to keep a fresh and lively interest in this flattest and emptiest of countries.

P.S. Tuesday.—The mail is in for once before the outward mail goes, and it brings yours of 1.10.15. What you report about Charles Lister is exactly what I should have expected. It is an element in all the best lives that their owners are reckless about throwing them away; but it's a little consolation to know that he didn't succeed exactly.

Most of my new letters are rather gloomy about the French offensive. We used gas and we're held up: and we're being diddled all round by kings in the Balkans.

Elton, by the way, was up at Balliol, a scholar 1911—and knows you, though whether individually or collectively I know not.

Also one Pirie of Exeter has come with the draft.

Amarah.

November 4, 1915.

To L.R.

I enclose an extract from a speech which might have been made by you, but was made by—who do you think? Our modern St. David.

I read Oliver's *Ordeal by Battle* before I left Agra. Most of my relations sent me a copy. So far only one has sent me A.J.B.'s *Theism and Humanism*: books are always welcome: but as their ultimate fate is very uncertain, it is wiser to stick to cheap ones.

I think the idea of R—— on an Economy League is too delicious. I should so like to hear the details of their economies.

I hope you have noticed the correspondence in The *Times* on Wild Birds and Fruit Growers, and that the latter contemplate invoking the aid of the Board of Agriculture in exterminating the former.

The birds here increase as the weather gets colder. Geese, duck and teal are to be seen flighting every day. We shot a pochard on Tuesday and a plover yesterday. Large flocks of night-herons visit the flood-lands and rooks have become common. White wagtails appeared in great numbers a few weeks ago, and sand-grouse are reported in vast numbers further north.

As there is no news, perhaps it would interest you to know, how we live in these billets.

The house is very convenient on the whole, though cold, as there is no glass in the large windows and the prevailing N.W. wind blows clean through, and there are no fire-places.

As to our mode of existence, my day is almost uniformly as follows:

6.30 *a.m.*	Am called and drink 1 cup cocoa and eat biscuits.
7.15 *a.m.*	Get up.

7.45 *a.m.*	Finished toilet and read *Times* till breakfast.
8.0	Breakfast. Porridge, scrambled eggs, bread and jam, tea.
8.30-9.15.	Read *Times*.
9.15-10.15.	Parade (or more often *not*, about twice a week 1 parade).
10.15-1.0	Read and write, unless interrupted by duties.
1.0	Lunch. Cold meat, pudding, cheese and bread, lemonade.
1.30-4.0.	Read and write.
4.0.	Tea, bread and jam.
4.30.	Censor Civil Telegrams.
4.45-6.15.	Take exercise, *e.g.*, walk, ride, fish, shoot, or play football.
6.15.	Have a bath.
6.30-7.30.	Play skat, or talk on verandah.
7.30.	Mess. Soup, fish, meat, veg., pudding, savoury, beer or whisky.
8.45-10.15	Bridge.
10.15.	Go to bed.

Such is the heroic existence of those who are bearing their country's burden in this remote and trying corner of the globe!

Enclosure.

"Meanwhile, let personal recrimination drop. It is the poison of all good counsel. In every controversy there are mean little men who assume that their own motives in taking up a line are of the most exalted and noble character, but that those who dare differ from them are animated by the basest personal aims. Such men are a small faction, but they are the mischief-makers that have many a time perverted discussion into dissension. Their aim seems to be to spread distrust and disunion amongst men whose co-operation is essential to national success. These creatures ought to be stamped out relentlessly by all parties as soon as they are seen crawling along the floor."

Amarah.

November 18, 1915.

To L.R.

As this week is Xmas mail, I have only time to wish you every blessing and especially those of peace and goodwill which are so sadly needed now.

I am dreadfully sorry to hear that S.'s cancer is reappearing. We need more of her sort just now. I pray that she may get over it, but there is no disease which leaves less hope.

I suppose everyone is struck by the weakness of a democracy in war time as compared with an autocracy like the German. It is a complaint as old as Demosthenes. But it does not shake my faith in democracy as the best form of Government, because mere strength and efficiency is not my ideal. If a magician were to offer to change us to-morrow into a state on the German model, I shouldn't accept the offer, not even for the sake of winning the war.

Amarah.

November 23, 1915.

To his Mother.

I strained a muscle in my leg at football yesterday and consequently can't put my foot to the ground at all to-day. It is a great nuisance as I'm afraid it will prevent my going on our little trek into the desert, which will probably come off next Monday.

The news of the fight at Suliman Pak came through yesterday morning and we had a holiday on spec, and a salute of twenty-one guns was ordered to be fired. The first effort at 8 a.m. was a ludicrous fiasco. The Volunteer Artillery, having no 'blank,' loaded the guns with charges of plain cordite. The result was that as each round was fired it made about as much noise as a shot-gun, and the packet of cordite would hop out of the barrel and burn peacefully on the ground ten yards away, like a Bengal match. Gorringe arrived in the middle in a fine rage, and stopped the show. I took a snapshot of him doing so which I hope will come out. He then ordered the salute to be fired at noon with live shell. This was quite entertaining. They ranged on the flood-land where we go after the geese, 3,700 yards: and it took the shells about ten seconds to get there. There were some Arab shepherds with their flocks between us and the water, and they didn't appear to enjoy it. They "scorned the sandy Libyan plain as one who wants to catch a train."

Thursday. As luck would have it, orders came round at 1 p.m. yesterday for half the Battalion (including A. Coy.) to move up-stream at once: and after an afternoon and evening of many flusters and changes of plan, they have just gone off this morning. My wretched leg prevents my going with them: but it is much better to-day and I hope to be able to go by the next boat. Destination is unknown but it can only be Kut or Baghdad: and I infer the latter from the facts (1) that Headquarters (C.O., Adjt. Q.M. etc.) have gone, which means that the other half Battalion is likely to follow shortly: and (2) that they won't want a whole Battalion at Kut. The scale of garrison out here is about as follows. Towns under 5,000 one Coy. or nothing, 5,000-10,000 two Coys. Over 10,000 a (nominal) Battalion: bar Basra where there are only three men and one boy. Baghdad being about 150,000 may reasonably require two Brigades or a Division. We haven't heard yet whether we've got Baghdad. They may even have more fighting to do, though most people don't think so.

I will try to cable before I go up.

The M.O. says I have slightly overstretched my calf-muscles. I jumped rather high at a bouncing ball while I was running: and I came down somehow with my left leg stuck out in such a way that the knee was bent the wrong way: and so overstretched the muscles at the back of the calf. But I can already walk with two sticks, and hope to be able to get on a boat in two or three days time. A week on the boat will give it a further rest.

Amarah.

December 1, 1915.

To his Mother.

Sophy's death affects me more than any since Goppa's. She was the most intimate of all my aunts, as I have constant memories of her from the earliest times I can remember till she went to live at Oxford. I was always devoted to her, and she had an almost uncanny power of reading my thoughts. I don't feel there can have been a shade of bitterness in death for her, though she loved life; but there is something woefully pathetic in its circumstances, the pain, the loneliness, the misery of the war.

I thought about her all yesterday. The sunset was the most wonderful I have seen out here, and it seemed to say that though God could be very terrible yet he was supremely tender and beautiful. How blank and futile a sunset would be to a consistent materialist, as A.J.B. points out in his lectures.

The result of publishing what he called my "hymn" in the *Times* of October 15th has been an application from an earnest Socialist for leave to print it on cards at 8*s.* 6*d.* a 1,000 to create a demand for an early peace! But I couldn't help focussing my thoughts of Sophy into these lines:

Strong Son of God is Love; and she was strong, For she loved much, and served; Rejoiced in all things human, only wrong Drew scorn as it deserved. Fair gift of God is faith: 'twas hers, to move The mountains, and ascend The Paradise of saints: which faith and love Made even Death her friend.

My leg is much better but will still keep me here some days, as I am not to go till fit to march. It is a great nuisance being unable to take exercise. I was in such splendid condition, and now I shall be quite soft again. However there are compensations. The others are only at Kut, which is as dull as this and much less comfortable;

and they have only 60lb. kits, which means precious little.

Swinburne I will begin when I feel stronger. The Golden Ass hasn't come. I ordered it years ago, before the war, to be sent on publication. It is a curious product of Latin decadence, about second century; the first notable departure from the classical style. The most celebrated thing in it is the story of Cupid and Psyche: didn't Correggio paint it round the walls of a palace in Rome? I went to see it with Sophy.

Amarah.

December 8, 1915.

To his Mother.

We are more cheerful now. In the first place we are less cold. The wind has dropped and we have devised various schemes for mitigating the excessive ventilation. I have hung two gaudy Arab rugs over my window, with a layer of *Times* between them and the bars. Some genius had an inspiration, acting on which we have pitched an E.P. tent in the mess room. It just fits and is the greatest success.

Finally, I sent my bearer to speculate in a charcoal brazier. This also is a great success. Three penn'orth of charcoal burns for ages and gives out any amount of heat; and there is no smell or smoke: far superior to any stove I've ever struck. So we live largely like troglodytes in darkness but comparative warmth. Between breakfast and tea one can sit on the sunny side of the verandah round the inner court, though all sunshine has still to be shared with the flies; but they're not the flies they were, more like English October flies.

Secondly, as far as we can see, the main troubles up stream are over. My account to Papa last mail was not very accurate, but I will write him the facts again, in the light of fuller information. Anyway they're back at Kut now, and ought to be able to look after themselves till our reinforcements come up. The first two boat-loads have arrived here this morning, and are pushing on. But it was a serious reverse and may have very bad effects here and in India and Persia unless it is promptly revenged.

Owing to the Salsette's grounding, there will be no mail this week.

My leg remains much the same. I can walk quite well with a slight limp but the doctor won't let me walk more than fifty yards. I am very thankful I was stopped from going up to Kut. "A" Coy. has been working at top pressure there, entrenching and putting up wire entanglements. And now they will have to stand a siege, on forty days' rations, till Younghusband and Gorringe can relieve them. So I should be very much *de trop* there. I always felt that my *entreé* into the football world should be pregnant with fate, and so it is proving.

I have been reading some Swinburne. He disappoints me as a mind-perverse, fantastic and involved. Obscure when he means something, he is worse when he means nothing. As an imagination he is wonderful. His poetry is really a series of vivid and crowding pictures only held together by a few general and loose, though big ideas. His style is marvellously musical but overweighted by his classical long-windedness and difficult syntax. Such a contrast to Tennyson where the idea shines out of the language which is so simple as to seem inevitable, and yet wonderfully subtle as well as musical.

Amarah.

December 12, 1915.

To R.K.

In the stress of the times I can't remember when I last wrote or what I said, so please forgive repetitions and obscurities.

Let me begin at November 24th, the day we heard of the victory at Ctesiphon or Sulman Pak. That afternoon I crocked my leg at footer and have been a hobbler ever since with first an elephantine calf and now a watery knee, which however, like the Tigris, gets less watery daily.

The very next day (November 25th) half the battalion, including my "A" Coy., was ordered up stream and departed next morning, leaving me fuming at the fancied missing of a promenade into Baghdad. But providence, as you may point out in your next sermon, is often kinder than it seems. Two days later I could just walk and tried to embark: but the M.T.O. stopped me at the last moment. (I have stood him a benedictine for this since.)

Meanwhile, events were happening up-river. The Press Bureau's account, I expect, compresses a great deal into "Subsequently our force took up a position lower down the river" or some such *façon de parler*. What happened was this. We attacked without reserves relying on the enemy having none. We have done it several times successfully: indeed our numbers imposed the necessity generally. This time there were reinforcements en route, had we waited. But I anticipate.

Well, we attacked, and carried their first line and half their second before darkness pulled us up. A successful day, though expensive in casualties. We bivouacked in their first line. Daybreak revealed the unpleasant surprise of strong enemy reinforcements, who are said to have diddled our spies by avoiding Baghdad: 5,000 of them. As we had started the affair about 12,000 strong to their 15,000, this was serious. They attacked and were driven off. In the afternoon they attacked again, in close formation: our artillery mowed them, but they came on and on, kept it up all night, with ever fresh reinforcements, bringing them to 30,000 strong all told. By dawn our men were exhausted and the position untenable. A retreat was ordered, that meant ninety miles back to Kut over a baked billiard table. The enemy pressed all the way. Once they surrounded our rear brigade. Two officers broke through their front lines to recall the front lot. Another evening we pitched a camp and left it empty to delay the enemy. Daily rearguard actions were fought. Five feverish days got us back to Kut, without disorder or great loss of men; but the loss in material was enormous. All possible supplies had been brought close up to the firing line to facilitate our pursuit: mainly in barges, the rest in carts. The wounded filled all the carts, so those supplies had to be abandoned. The Tigris is a cork-screwed maze of mud-banks, no river for the hasty withdrawal of congested barges under fire. You can imagine the scene. Accounts differ as to what we lost. *Certainly*, two gunboats (destroyed), one monitor (disabled and captured), the telegraph barge and supply barge, besides all supplies, dumped on the bank. Most accounts add one barge of sick and wounded (400), the aeroplane barge, and a varying number of supply barges. In men from first to last we lost nearly 5,000: the Turks about 9,000—a guess of course.

The tale of woe is nearly complete. My "A" Coy. got as far as Kut and was set to feverish entrenching and wiring. Now the whole force there, some 8,000 in all, is cut off there and besieged. They have rations (some say half rations) for six weeks or two months, and ammunition. They are being bombarded, and have been attacked once, but repelled it easily. We aren't worried about them; but I with my leg (like another egoist) can't be sorry to be out of it. I should like to be there to mother my men. Our Major is wounded and the other officers infants; the Captain a Colonial one I'm glad to say.

Meanwhile our reinforcements have turned up in great numbers and expect to be able to relieve Kut by the end of the month. I mustn't particularise too much. In fact I doubt whether this or any letters will be allowed to go through this week. The men are warned only to write postcards. The dear censor has more excuse where Indians are concerned. I can walk short walks now. Life is rather slow, but I have several books luckily.

Amarah.

December 20, 1915.

To N.B.

There is a double mail to answer this week and only two days to do it in, so this may be rather hurried.

I do get the *Round Table*. I don't think it suggests a World State as practical politics, but merely as the only ideal with which the mind can be satisfied as an ultimate end. If you believe in a duty to all humanity, logic won't stop short of a political brotherhood of the world, since national loyalty implies in the last resort a denial of your duty to everyone outside your nation. But in fact, of course, men are influenced by sentiment and not logic: and I agree that, for ages to come at least, a World State wouldn't inspire loyalty. I don't even think the British Empire would for long, if it relied only on the sentiment of the Mother Country as home. The loyalty of each Dominion to the Empire in future generations will be largely rooted in its own distinctive nationalism, paradoxical as that sounds: at least so I believe.

Please don't refrain from comments on passing events for fear they will be stale. They aren't, because my *Times's* are contemporary with your letters: and the amount of news we get by Reuter's is negligible. Indeed Reuter's chiefly enlighten us as to events in Mesopotamia. Last night we heard that Chamberlain had announced in the House that the Turks lost 2,000 and the Arabs 1,000 in the attack on Kut on December 12th: that was absolutely the first we'd heard of it, though Kut is only ninety miles as the crow flies, and my Company is there! All we hear is their casualties, thrice a week. They now total 2 killed and 11 wounded out of 180: nearly all my Company and 3 of my draft wounded.

I want to be there very much, to look after them, poor dears: but I must say that T.A's view that a place like Kut is desirable to be in *per se* never fails to amaze me, familiar though it now is. I had another instance of it last night. About twelve of my draft were left behind on various duties when the Coy. went up-river in such a hurry. Hearing that my knee was so much better they sent me a deputy to ask me to make every effort to take them with me if I went up-river. I agreed, of course, but what, as usual, struck me was that the motives I can understand—that one's duty is with the Coy. when there's trouble around, or even that it's nicer to be with one's pals at Kut than lonely at Amarah—didn't appear at all. The two things he kept harping on were (1) it's so dull to miss a "scrap" and (2) there may be a special clasp given for Kut, and we don't want to miss it. They evidently regard the Coy. at Kut as lucky dogs having a treat: the "treat" when analysed (which they don't) consisting of 20lb. kits in December, half-rations, more or less regular bombardment, no proper billets, no shops, no letters, and very hard work!

My leg is very decidedly better now. I can walk half-a-mile without feeling any aches, and soon hope to do a mile. There is an obstinate little puffy patch which won't disappear just beside the knee-cap: but the M.O. says I may increase my walk each day up to the point where it begins to ache.

We have had no rain here for nearly a month; but there are light clouds about which make the most gorgeous sunsets I ever saw.

Extract from Letter to his Mother.

December, 1915.

I am looking forward to this trek. Four months is a large enough slice of one's time to spend in Amarah, and there will probably be more interest and fewer battles on this trek than could be got on any other front. The Censor has properly got the breeze up here, so I probably shan't be able to tell you anything of our movements or to send you any wires: but I will try and let you hear something each week; and if we are away in the desert, we generally arrange—and I will try to—for some officer who is within reach of the post to write you a line saying I am all right (which he hears by wireless) but can't write. That is what we have been doing for the people at Kut. But there are bound to be gaps, and they will tend to get more frequent and longer as we get further.

No casualties from "A" Coy. for several days: so I hope its main troubles are over.

Extract of Letter to P.C.

Xmas Day, 1915.

... I'm so glad Gwalior was a success. I think a good native state is the most satisfactory kind of Government for India in many ways; but (a) so few are really good, if you go behind the scenes and think of such fussy things as security of life and property, taxation and its proportion to benefits received, justice and administration, education, freedom of the subject, and so on. (b) It spells stagnation and the abandonment of the hope of training the mass of the people to responsibility; but I think that is an academic rather than practical point at present.

Christmas is almost unbearable in war-time: the pathos and the reproach of it. I am thankful that my Company is at Kut on half-rations. I don't of course mean that: but I'm thankful to be spared eating roast beef and plum pudding heartily, as these dear pachyderms are now doing with such relish. I'm glad they do, and I'd do it too if my Company was here. I'm always thankful for my thin skin, but I'm glad dear God made thick ones the rule in this wintry world.

Amarah.

Extract from letter to N.B.

It seems odd to get just now your letter answering my arguments *against* the advance to Baghdad. They were twofold (1) Military, that we should not have the force to hold it and our communications would be too vulnerable. These objections have been largely met (*a*) by large reinforcements, which will nearly double our forces when they are all up, (*b*) by the monitors—the second is here now; they solve the communication problem. I think now it will take a fresh Army Corps from Constantinople to dislodge us: and I now hear that the difficulties of *its* communications would be very great. (2) Politically. I thought the occupation of Baghdad would cause trouble (*a*) with Russia, (*b*) with Indian soldiers, (*c*) with Moslems generally. Here again (*a*) P. tells me Russia is giving us a free hand, (*b*) trouble did occur with some Indian Regiments, but it took the mild form of a strike, and the disaffected units have been dispersed by Coys. over the lines of communication. (*c*) As regards Moslems in India, I think I was wrong. The bold course, even to bluffing, generally pays with

Orientals. We have incurred their resentment by fighting Turkey and on the whole we had better regain their respect by beating her. Of course we shall respect their religious feelings and prejudices in every practicable way.

Amarah.

December 26, 1915.

To M.H.

I hope you safely received the MS. I sent you last mail.

Orders to move have interrupted my literary activities, and I shall have to spend the few days before we start chiefly in testing the fitness of my leg for marching. I went shooting on Friday and walked about six miles quite successfully, bar a slight limp; and I mean to extend progressively up to twelve.

The weather has suddenly turned wet, introducing us to a new vileness of the climate. I hope it won't last— it means unlimited slime.

I shan't be able to write much or often for some time, I expect, as we shall be marching pretty continuously, I reckon. I shall try and write to Ma and Pa at each opportunity, and to you if there's time and paper available. Your little writing-block may come in handy.

One of my draft has been killed and five wounded at Kut. Our casualties there are 21 out of 180. I shall look forward to seeing my men again: I hope about the second Sunday after Epiphany. We shall then march with a force equal to the King of France's on his celebrated and abortive expedition of ascent. Our destination is a profound secret, but you may give Nissit three guesses and make her write me her answers on a Valentine.

Christmas passed off quietly and cheerfully. T.A. is so profoundly insensible of incongruities that he saw nothing to worry him in the legend A Merry Christmas and the latest casualty list on the same wall of the R.A.T.A. room: and he sang "Peace on earth and mercy mild" and "Confound their politics" with equal gusto. And his temper is infectious while you're with him.

The most perplexing Reuter's come through from the Balkans.

Amarah.

Christmas Day, 1915.

To R.K.

I hope you got my last letter safely. I enclosed it in my home one to be forwarded.

There is little news from this theatre, and what there is we mayn't write, for the most part.

My Coy. is being bombarded at Kut still. They have had 21 casualties out of 180. One of my draft is killed and five wounded and here everyone is parroting about a Merry Christmas. Truly the military man is a pachyderm.

This is likely to be the last you will hear of me for some time, though I hope to be able to dob out a post-card here and there, perhaps letters now and then. In a word, we're moving next week and are not likely to see billets again till we lodge with the descendants, either of the Caliphs or of Abraham's early neighbours.

My leg is so far recovered that I take it as almost certain I shall march too when we go. I am testing it to make sure first. Yesterday it did six miles without damage, though the gait remains Hephaestian.

The weather is still cold, and fine and dry. The sunsets are glorious.

Amarah.

December 26, 1915.

To N.B.

Christmas and submarines have made the mails very late and we have again been nearly a fortnight without any.

We have got our orders to move and so I look forward to a fairly prolonged period of trekking, during which it will hardly be possible to do more than write odd postcards and occasional short letters; but I will write when I can. We start in two or three days time.

I expect my leg will be all right for marching. When I heard we were moving, I went to the hospital to consult the chief M.O. there about it. He examined *both* my legs gravely and then firmly grasping the sound one pronounced that it had still an excess of fluid in it: which I take to be a sincere though indirect tribute to the subsidence of the fluid in the crocked one. He proceeded to prescribe an exactly reverse treatment to that recommended by the other M.O., which had the advantage of giving me official sanction for pretty well anything I chose to do or not do. The upshot of it was that I decided to test the old leg for myself to determine whether it was fit for marching or not. So I began with a six mile walk on Friday, shooting: and found that my graceful limb did not impede my progress nor develop into any graver symptoms. I was more tired than I should have been a month ago, but that was natural. Yesterday was monopolised by Christmas functions; to-day I mean to try eight or nine miles, and ten or twelve to-morrow. If the thing is going to crock it had better do it before I start: but it shows no sign of it.

The latest way of indicating latitude and longitude is like a date, *e.g.* 32.25/44/10: you can take the N. and E. for granted.

It has most tactlessly begun to rain again to-day, and with an E. wind it may continue, which will mean a vile slime for marching.

The Christmas sports were really great fun: one of them—one-minute impromptu speeches—would make quite a good house-party game.

P.S.—You must think me brutal not to have mentioned my poor men. I have written so many letters this morning, I didn't notice it in this one. They are still being bombarded and have had 21 casualties out of 180: 5 killed, one of my draft, 2 officers slightly wounded. I hope to see them about Twelfth Night—no, say second Sunday after Epiphany!

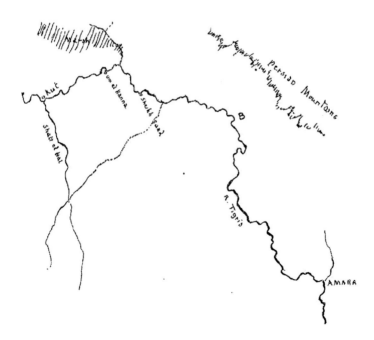

Camp.

January 3, 1916.

To P.C.

... That afternoon the new draft arrived, headed by Jack Stillwell and Lester Garland. They arrived only 45 strong, having reached Basra over 100. Basra is a nest of military harpies who seize men for obscure duties and make them local sergts. Only 68 escaped from it; and of these 23 fell out on the march—another specimen of R.A.M.C. efficiency. The M.O. at Quetta had merely passed down the line asking each man "Are you fit?" and taking his answer.

In this letter A. stands for Amarah, C. for Kut, B. for Ali Gherbi.

B.

Sunday, January 2, 1916.

To his Father.

As I shan't be able to mention places in connection with our movements, I shall call the station we left on December 31st A., this place B. and so on; and I think you ought to be able to follow, as I will make the lettering consistent.

We left A. at 2 p.m. on Friday. The men were on barges slung on either side of the river-boat, on which various details, our officers and the General and his staff were.

I brought my gun and 150 cartridges, and was unexpectedly soon rewarded: for one of the A.C.C's staff came along after lunch and asked for someone to come with him in the motor-boat and shoot partridges. As I was the only one with a gun handy I went. We raced ahead in the motor-boat for half-an-hour and then landed on the right bank and walked up the river for two-and-a-half hours, not deviating even to follow up coveys. There were a lot of birds, but it was windy and they were wild and difficult. Also with only two guns and three sepoys we walked over as many as we put up. Craik (the A.D.C's name, he is an Australian parson in peace-time) was a poor performer and only accounted for three. I got thirteen, a quail, a plover and a hare. I missed three or four sitters and lost two runners, but on the whole shot quite decently, as the extreme roughness of the hard-baked ploughed (or rather mattocked) land is almost more of an obstacle to good shooting than the behaviour of the birds. Craik was a stayer, and as the wind dropped at sunset and the birds grew tamer he persevered till it was dark. Then we had to walk three-quarters-of-a-mile before we could find a place where the boat could get in near the bank: so we had a longer and colder chase to catch up the ship than I had bargained for, especially as I had foolishly forgotten to bring a coat. However, when I got too cold I snuggled up against the engine and so kept parts of me warm. Luckily the ship had to halt at the camp of a marching column, so we caught her up in one-and-a-quarter hours.

I pitched my bed on deck up against the boiler, and so was as warm as toast all night.

Yesterday morning we steamed steadily along through absolutely bare country. The chief feature was the extraordinary abundance of sand-grouse. I told Mamma of the astonishing clouds of them which passed over A. Here they were in small parties or in flocks up to 200: but the whole landscape is dotted with them from 8 a.m. till 11 and again from 3 to 4: so that any random spot would give one much the same shooting as we had at the Kimberley dams. An officer on board told me that when he was here two months ago, a brother officer had killed fifty to his own gun: and a Punjabi subaltern got twenty-one with five shots.

We reached here about 2 p.m. This place is only about forty-five miles from A. as the crow flies, but by river it takes sixteen hours, and with various halts and delays it took us just twenty-four. We only ran on to one mud-bank. The effect was curious. The ship and the port barge stopped dead though without any shock. The starboard barge missed the mud and went on, snapping the hawsers and iron cables uniting us. The only visible sign of the bank was an eddying of the current over it: it was right in midstream.

This is a most desolate place. Apart from the village with its few palms and gardens there seems not to be a blade of vegetation within sight. To the N.E. the Persian hills are only fifteen miles away. They have still a little snow (did I mention that the storm which gave us rain at A. had capped these hills with a fine snow mantle?)

Here we found "D" Co., which got stranded here when "A" Co. got stuck in C. We are about forty-five or fifty miles from C. as the crow flies, and the guns can be heard quite plainly: but things have been very quiet the last few days. There is an enemy force of 2,000 about ten miles from here, but how long they and the ones at C. will wait remains to be seen.

We know nothing of our own movements yet and I couldn't mention them if we did. We have been put into a different brigade, but the brigadier has not been appointed yet. The number of the brigade equals that of the ungrateful lepers or the bean-rows which Yeats intended to plant at Innisfree. We are independent of any division.

A mysterious Reuter has come through about conscription. As it quotes the *Westminster* as saying Asquith has decided on it, I'm inclined to believe it: but it goes on to talk obscurely of possible resignations and a general election.

This may catch the same mail as my letter to Mamma from A.

P.S. Please tell Mamma that just as we were embarking, the S. and T. delivered me two packages, which turned out to be the long-lost blue jerseys. So there is hope for the fishing rods yet.

Monday, January 10, 1915.

To his Mother.

I will use a spare hour to begin an account of our doings since I last wrote, but I don't know when I shall be able to finish it, still less when post it.

We left B. last Thursday morning and were told we should march sixteen miles: we marched up the right bank, so our left flank was exposed to the desert, and "D" Company did flank guard. My platoon formed the outer screen and we marched strung out in single file. There were cavalry patrols beyond us again, and anyway no Arab could come within five miles without our seeing him, so our guarding was a sinecure.

We paraded as soon as it was light, at 7.15 a.m., but owing to the transport delays, the column did not start till after 9.0. The transport consists of: (a) ships and barges; (b) carts, mules and camels. Each has its limitations. Ships tie you to the river-bank, so every column must have some land transport. Camels can hardly move after rain: they slip and split themselves. The carts are fearfully held up by the innumerable ditches which are for draining the floods back to the river. There are not nearly enough mules to go round and they only carry 160lbs. each. So you can imagine our transport difficulties. The country supplies neither food, fodder nor fuel. Our firewood comes from India. If you leave the river you must carry every drop of drinking water. So the transport line was three times as long as the column itself, and moved more slowly.

Our new Brigadier turned up and proved to be a pleasant, sensible kind of man, looking rather like Lord Derby. Having just come from France, he keeps quite cool whatever we encounter. (P.S. We have had a new Brigadier since this one, I haven't yet seen the present one.)

The march was slow and rough, as most of the ground was hard-baked plough. The country was as level and bare as a table, bar the ditches, and we hardly saw a human being all day. It took us till after 4 p.m. to do our sixteen miles. About 2 p.m. we began to hear firing and see shrapnel in the distance, and it soon became clear that we were approaching a big battle. Consequently we had to push on beyond our sixteen miles, and went on till Sunset. By this time we were all very footsore and exhausted. The men had had no food since the night before, the ration-cart having stuck in a ditch; and many of the inexperienced ones had brought nothing with them. My leg held out wonderfully well, and in fact has given me no trouble worth speaking of.

We had to wait an hour for orders, the Brigadier knowing nothing of the General's intentions. By six it was quite dark, and the firing had ceased: and we got orders to retrace our steps to a certain camping place (marked *I* on sketch). This meant an extra mile, and immense trouble and confusion in finding our way over ditches and then sorting kits in the dark: but finally we did it, ate a meal, and turned in about 9.30 p.m. pretty well tired out, as we had been on the move fourteen hours and had marched about twenty-one miles. To put the lid on it, a sharp shower of exceedingly frigid rain surprised us all in our beauty sleep, about 11 p.m. and soaked the men's blankets and clothes. Luckily I had everything covered up, and I spread my overcoat over my head and slept on, breathing through the pocket-holes.

(I will continue this in diary form and post it if and when I get a chance.)

Friday 7th. Started at 8.30 and marched quietly about five miles. This brought us within view of the large village of D., which is roughly half-way between B. and C. Between us and it the battle was in full swing. We halted by a pontoon bridge (2 on sketch), just out of range of the enemy's guns, and watched it for several hours. Owing to the utter flatness of the ground, we could see very little of the infantry. It was hot and the mirage blurred everything. Our artillery was clearly very superior to theirs, both in quantity (quite five to one it seemed) and in the possession of high explosive shell, of which the enemy had none: but we were cruelly handicapped (*a*) by the fact that their men and guns were entrenched and ours exposed; and (*b*) by the mirage, which made the location of their trenches and emplacements almost impossible.

I had better not say much about the battle yet, but I will give a rough sketch and describe our own experiences. I will only say this, that the two great difficulties our side had to contend with were: (1) the inability of the artillery to locate anything with certainly in the mists and mirage, and (2) the difficulty of finding and getting round the enemy's flanks. Either they had a far larger force than we expected, or they were very skilfully spread out—for they covered an amazingly wide front, quite eight miles, I should say, or more.

The battle was interesting to watch, but not exciting. The noise of the shells from field guns is exactly like that of a rocket going up. When the shell is coming towards you, there is a sharper hiss in it, like a whip. It gives you a second or two to get under cover and then crack-whizz as the shrapnel whizzes out. The heavy shells from the monitors, etc., make a noise more like a landslide of pebbles down a beach, only blurred as if echoed. Bobbety's "silk dress swishing through the air" does his imagination credit, but is not quite accurate, nor does it express the spirit of the things quite!

About 3.30 we had orders to cross to the left bank. As we passed over the bridge, we put up two duck, who had been swimming there peacefully with the shells flying over their heads every half minute for hours. When we reached the left bank we marched as if to reinforce our right flank. Presently the Brigadier made us line out into echelon of companies in line in single rank, so that from a distance we looked like a brigade, instead of three companies. About 4 we came up to a howitzer battery and lay down about 200 yards from it, thus:

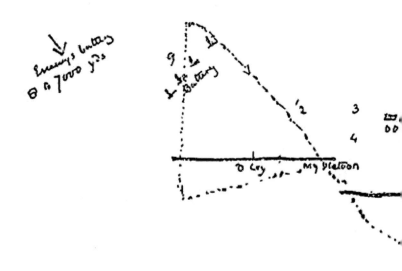

We had lain there about ten minutes when a hiss, crack, whizz, and shells began to arrive, invariably in pairs, about where I've put the 1 and 2. We had a fine view. The first notice we had of each shell was the sudden appearance of a white puff, about thirty feet above ground, then a spatter of dust about thirty yards to the right, then the hiss-crack-whizz. They were ranging on the battery, but after a minute or two they spotted the ammunition column, and a pair of shells burst at 3, then a pair at 4. So the column retreated in a hurry along the dotted arrow, and the shells following them began to catch us in enfilade. So Foster made us rise and move to the left in file. Just as we were up, a pair burst right over my platoon. I can't conceive why nobody was hit. I noticed six bullets strike the ground in a semi-circle between me and the nearest man three paces away, and everyone else noticed the same kind of thing, but nobody was touched. I don't suppose the enemy saw us at all: anyway, the next pair pitched 100 yards beyond us, following the mules, and wounded three men in C. Company: and the next got two men of B.—all flesh wounds and not severe. They never touched the ammunition column.

We lay down in a convenient ditch, and only one more pair came our way, as the enemy was ranging back to the battery. Of this pair, one hit the edge of the ditch and buried itself without exploding, and the other missed with its bullets, while the case bounced along and hit a sergeant on the backside, not even bruising it.

Just before 5 we got orders to advance in artillery formation. My platoon led, and we followed a course shown by the dotted line. We went through the battery and about 300 yards beyond, and then had orders to return to camp. On this trip (which was mere window-dressing) no shell came nearer than fifty yards: in fact our own battery made us jump much more.

The whole episode was much more interesting than alarming. Fear is seated in the imagination, I think, and vanishes once the mind can assert itself. One feels very funky in the cold nights when nothing is happening: but if one has to handle men under fire, one is braced up and one's attention is occupied. I expect rifle fire is much more trying: but the fact that shell-fire is more or less unaimed at one individually, and also the warning swish, gives one a feeling of great security.

We got back to camp near the river (4 on sketch) about 6, and dug a perimeter, hoping to settle down for the night. But at 7.30 orders came to move at 9.30. We were told that an enemy force had worked round our right flank, and that our brigade had to do a night march eastward down the river and attack it at dawn. So at 10 p.m. we marched with just a blanket apiece, leaving our kits in the camp. After we had gone, the Q.M. made up a big fire and got in no fewer than fifty-two wounded, who were trying to struggle back to the field dressing station from the firing line four or five miles away.

The fire attracted them and parties went out to help them in. I think it is very unsatisfactory that beyond the regimental stretcher-bearers there is no ambulance to bring the wounded back: and how can a dozen stretchers convey 300 casualties five miles? It is a case of *sauve qui peut* for the wounded: and when they get to the dressing station the congestion is very bad, thirty men in a tent, and only three or four doctors to deal with 3,000 or 4,000 wounded. I mention this as confirming my previous criticism of the medical service here.

Well, we started out at 10 p.m. and marched slowly and silently till nearly midnight. Then we bivouacked for four-and-a-half-hours (5 on sketch,) and a more uncomfortable time I hope never to spend. We had not dared bring rugs for fear of losing them in the subsequent attack, so I had nothing but my Burberry, a muffler and a woollen helmet. The ground was bare earth everywhere, very damp and cold. I lay in a ditch and slept for three-quarters-of-an hour, and then woke with extremely cold feet, so I walked about a little, and then, finding Foster in the same case, we both took off our Burberrys and laid one under us and one above and lay like babes in the wood. This expedient kept one flank nicely warm, and soon I got North to make a pillow of my other thigh, which kept *that* warm: but from the knees downwards I was incurably cold and never got to sleep again. The men were better off, having each a blanket, and sleeping in packets of four.

Saturday. At last 4.30 a.m. arrived and we started marching again. It was a blessing to get one's feet warm but the pleasures of the march were strictly comparative. We trekked on eastwards along the river-bank till sunrise, 7 a.m., when we came on a camp of Arabs who fled shrieking at our approach (6 on sketch.) At 7.30, we halted and had breakfast. Our united efforts failed to find enough fuel to boil a kettle. We waited till 9, when the cavalry patrols returned and reported no sign of the enemy, so we marched back to the pontoon bridge (7 on sketch). I suspect our re-entry *qua* stage reinforcements was the whole object of our expedition, and the out-flankers were a myth from the beginning. The march back was the most unpleasant we've had. It got hot and the ground was hard and rough and we were all very tired and footsore. A sleepless night takes the stamina out of one. There and back our trek was about twelve miles.

On arrival at the bridge we were only allowed half-an-hour's rest and then got orders to march out to take up an 'observation post' on the right flank. Being general reserve is no sinecure with bluffing tactics prevailing.

This last lap was extremely trying. We marched in artillery formation, all very lame and stiff. We passed behind our yesterday's friend, the howitzer battery, but at a more respectful distance from the enemy's battery. This latter showed no sign of life till we were nearly two miles from the river. Then it started its double deliveries and some of them came fairly close to some of our platoon, but not to mine.

It took us nearly two hours to drag ourselves three miles and the men had hardly a kick in them when we reached the place assigned for our post (8 on sketch). We were ordered to entrench in echelon of companies facing North. I thought it would take till dark to get us dug in (it was 2 p.m.); but luckily our men, lined up ready to begin digging, caught the eye of the enemy as a fine enfilade target (or else they saw our first line mules) and they started shelling us from 6,500 yards (Enemy's battery, 9 on sketch). The effect on the men was magical. They woke up and dug so well that we had fair cover within half an hour and quite adequate trenches by 3. This bombardment was quite exciting. The first few pairs were exactly over "D" Company's trench, but pitched about 100 yards beyond it. The next few were exactly right in range, but about forty yards right, *i.e.* behind us. Just as we were wondering where the third lot would be, our faithful howitzer battery and some heavy guns behind them, which opened all they knew on the enemy battery as soon as they opened on us, succeeded in attracting its fire to themselves. This happened three or four times. Just as they were getting on to us the artillery saved us: there would be a sharp artillery duel and then the Turks would lie quiet for ten minutes, then begin on us again. This went on until we were too well dug in to be a tempting target, and they devoted themselves to our battery. The curious part of it was that though we could see the flash of their guns every time, the mirages made it impossible to judge their ranges or even for our battery to observe its own fire properly. Our howitzer battery unfortunately was not in a mirage, and they had its range to a yard and plastered it with shrapnel. If they had had high explosives they could have smashed it.

About 4.30 the mirage cleared and our guns had a free go for the first time that day: (in the morning mists last until the mirage begins). I'm told the mirage had put our guns over 1,000 yards out in their ranging, but I doubt this. Anyway it is the fact that those guns and trenches which were sited in mirages were practically untouched in a heavy two days' bombardment.

In that last hour, however, between 4.20 and dark, our heavy guns got into the enemy finely with their high explosives. They blew one of our tormentors bodily into the air at 10,500 yards, and silenced the others, and chased every Turk out of the landscape.

All the same, we were rather gloomy that night. Our line had made no progress that we could hear of; we had had heavy losses (none in our battalion), and there seemed no prospect of dislodging the enemy. Their front was so wide we could not get round them, and frontal attacks on trenches are desperate affairs here if your artillery is paralysed by mirages. The troops who have come from France say that in this respect this action has been more trying than either Neuve Chappelle or Ypres, because, as they say, it is like advancing over a billiard-table all the way.

To crown our troubles, we were three miles from the river, which meant no water except for necessities—the men had no kits, and it was very cold, and we could not show lights. And finally, after midnight, it began to pour with rain!

Sunday. At 5.30 we stood to arms. It rained harder than ever and most of us hadn't a dry stitch. At last it got light, the rain gradually stopped, and a thoroughly depressed battalion breakfasted in a grey mist, expecting to be bombarded the moment it lifted. About 8.30 the mist cleared a little, and we looked in vain for our tormentors. Our cavalry reconnoitred and, to our joy, we saw them ride clean over the place where the enemy's line had been the evening before. They had gone in the night.

A cold but drying wind sprang up and the sun came out for a short time, and we managed to get our things dry. At 1 o'clock we marched back to the river and found the bridge gone.

I think this makes a good place to stop, as it marks the end of our first series of adventures and of the no doubt by now famous battle of D.

I enclose a sketch-map to explain our movements. For obvious reasons I can't say much about the battle itself.

(I will briefly bring this up to date, post it and try to get a cable through to you.)

When we reached the river (10 on sketch), it began to rain again and we spent a very chill and damp afternoon on the bank awaiting orders. About dusk B. and C. Companies were ordered to cross the river to guard the hospital there, and D. stayed to guard the hospital on the left bank. Mercifully our ship was handy, so we got our tents and slept warm, though all our things were wettish.

Monday. A quiet morning, no orders. A Scotch mist shrouded everything till noon and kept our things damp, but the sun got through at last.

C. Company returned to left bank, as all wounded were being shipped across. (N.B. They had to bring them across in our ship. There is still no sign of the Red Cross motor boats up *here*, though I'm glad to hear they've reached Basra.) We got orders to march to D. by night. We started at 8 p.m., "B." Company marching parallel on the other bank. It was seven or eight miles, but we went very slow, and did not get in till 1.30 and our transport not till nearly 3, heavy guns sticking in the ditches. (N.B. Once we got behind the evacuated Turkish line, we found that the ditches had been filled in to allow passage of guns, an expedient which had apparently not occurred to the British Command, for no ditch had been filled in between B, and this point!)

Tuesday. When morning came we found ourselves camped just opposite D. (11 on sketch), and we are still there. Two fine days (though it freezes at night) and rest have restored us. A mail arrived this morning, bringing letters to December 7th, and your medical parcels.

I only returned you the quinine and bandages, of which people in Amara have plenty. They will come in handy for you to send out again. *Here* everything medical can be used, but I couldn't have brought any more than I did. As it is, I've left a lot at Amarah.

I must close now. On these cold nights the little kitchener is invaluable, so is the soup. Of the various brands you sent, Ivelcon is the best. The chocolate is my mainstay on day marches. Also the Diet Tablets are very good. Bivouac Cocoa is also good. The Kaross is invaluable.

Stanford's Map has arrived.

MAP ENCLOSED IN LETTER OF JAN. 10.

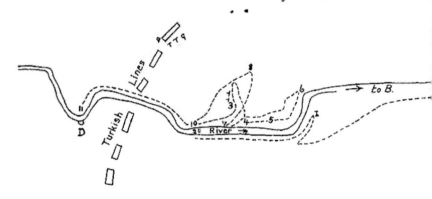

On the E. Canal.

Saturday, January 15th, 1916.

To his Mother.

I will continue my account of our doings in diary form.
Last week we had a kind of general introduction to war.

The last few days we have seen a few of its more gruesome details.

12th, Wednesday. After posting your letter and one to Luly I read some of the Mail's papers. We have had absolutely no outside news since January 1st, and get very little even of the operations of our own force. I then went to see Foster who has had to go sick and lives on our supply ship. About 20 per cent. of our men are sick, mostly diarrhœa and sore feet. The former is no doubt due to Tigris water. They don't carry the chlorinating plant on trek, and men often have to replenish water-bottles during short halts. Personally I have so far avoided unboiled water. I have my bottle filled with tea before leaving camp, and can make that last me forty-eight hours, and eke it out with soup or cocoa in the Little Kitchener at bivouacs.

In the evening "D." Company had to find a firing party to shoot three Indians, two N.C.Os. and one sepoy, for cowardice in the face of the enemy. I'm thankful that North and not I was detailed for the job. I think there is nothing more horrible in all war than these executions. Luckily they are rare. The men, however, didn't mind at all. I talked to the corporal about it afterwards—a particularly nice and youthful one, one of my draft—and remarked that it was a nasty job for him to have to do. to which he replied gaily, "Well, sir, I 'ad a bit o' rust in my barrel wanted shootin' out, so it came in handy like." T.A. is a wonderful and attractive creature.

13th, Thursday. Moved at 7 a.m., carrying food and water for two days. The enemy had been located on the E. Canal, about eight miles from D., and our people were going to attack them. The idea was to hold them in front with a small force, while a much bigger force got round their left flank (the Canal is on the left bank of the river). Our brigade was to support the frontal containing force.

We marched about four miles and then halted about 9 a.m. There was a strong and cold S.E. wind blowing, which prevented our hearing any firing, and we could see very little shelling. Our air plane first reported that a certain fort, which stood about a mile in advance of the enemy's left flank, was strongly held; but we seem to have shelled them out of that pretty easily, for about 2 p.m. it reported again that the enemy had left his trenches on the Canal.

About 3.30 p.m. we advanced, and reached the aforesaid fort a little before sunset. Here we heard various alarming and depressing reports, the facts underlying which, as far as I can make out at present, were these.

The Turks, seeing their left flank being turned, quitted their position and engaged the outflanking force, leaving only about 500 out of their 9,000 to hold the canal. Our outflanking force, finding itself heavily engaged, sent and asked the frontal force to advance, to relieve the pressure. The frontal force, hearing at the same time that the Turks had quitted their Canal trenches, advanced too rashly and were surprised and heavily punished by the remnant left along the Canal, losing half their force and being obliged to retire. So when they met us they naturally gave us the impression that there was a large force still holding the Canal, which we should have to tackle in the morning.

We dug ourselves in about 2,000 yards from the Canal. It was very cold and windy, and we had not even a blanket, though I had luckily brought both my greatcoat and Burberry. There was a small mud hut just behind our trench, littered with Turkish rags. The signallers made a fire inside, and two stray Sikhs had rolled themselves up in a corner. It was not an inviting spot, but it was a choice between dirt and cold, and I had no hesitation in choosing dirt. So after a chill dinner, at which I drank neat lime-juice and neat brandy alternately (to save my water-bottle intact), I turned into the hut. The other officers (except North) at first disdained it with disgust, but as the night wore on they dropped in one by one, till by midnight we were lying in layers like sardines. The Colonel was the last to surrender. I have a great admiration for him. He is too old for this kind of game, and feels the cold and fatigue very much: but he not only never complains, but is always quietly making the best of things for everyone and taking less than his share of anything good that is going. Nothing would induce him, on this occasion, to lie near the fire.

14th, Friday. The night having passed more pleasantly than could have been expected, we stood to arms in the trenches at 5.30 a.m. This is a singularly unpleasing process, especially when all you have to look forward to is the prospect of attacking 9,000 Turks in trenches behind a Canal! But one's attention is fully occupied in trying to keep warm.

As soon as it was light we got orders to advance and marched in artillery formation to within 1,200 yards of the Canal, where we found some hastily begun trenches of the day before, and proceeded to deepen them. As there was no sign of the enemy, the conviction grew on us that he must have gone in the night; and presently the order came to stop entrenching and form a line to clear up the battlefield, *i.e.* the space between us and the Canal. This included burying the dead and picking up wounded, as the stretcher parties which had tried to bring the wounded in during the night had been heavily fired on and unable to get further than where we were.

I had never seen a dead man and rather dreaded the effect on my queasy stomach; but when it came to finding, searching and burying them one by one, all sense of horror—though they were not pleasant to look upon—was forgotten in an overmastering feeling of pity, such as one feels at the tragic ending of a moving story, only so oppressive as to make the whole scene like a sad and impersonal dream, on which and as in a dream my mind kept recurring to a tableau which I must have seen over fifteen years ago in Madame Tussaud's of Edith finding the body of Harold after the battle of Hastings, and indeed the stiff corpses were more like waxen models than anything that had lived.

The wounded were by comparison a cheerful company, though their sufferings during the eighteen hours they had lain there must have been fearful: but the satisfaction of being able to bring them in was our predominant feeling.

In the middle of this work we were suddenly recalled and ordered to march to the support of the outflanking force, of whose movements we had heard absolutely nothing. But when we had fallen in, all they did was to march us to the Canal, and thence along it back to the river, where we encamped about 1 p.m. and still are.

It was a great comfort to be within reach of water again, though the wind and rain have made the river so muddy that a mug of water from it looks exactly like a mug of tea with milk in it.

The wind had continued unabated for two days and now blew almost a gale. The dust was intolerable and made any attempts at washing hopeless. Indeed one's eyes got so full of it the moment they were opened that we sat blinking like owls or shut them altogether. So it was a cheerless afternoon, with rain threatening. Our supply ship with our tents had not come up, but the Major (Stillwell) had a bivouac tent on the second line transport, which he invited me to share, an offer which I gladly accepted. We made it as air-tight as possible, and built a wall of lumps of hard-baked mud to protect us from snipers, and slept quite reasonably warm. It came on to rain heavily in the night, so I was lucky to be under shelter.

15th, Saturday. This morning it rained on and off till nearly noon, and the wind blew all day and the sun never got properly through: but the rain had laid the dust.

N.B.—With regard to parcels, none are arriving now, just when they're wanted. The fact is they have to economise their transport most rigidly. A staff officer told me that our supply of river-boats just enables one boat (with its pair of barges alongside) to reach us every day; our food for one day fills one entire barge, so that you can imagine there is not much room to spare after ammunition and other war material has been put on board. The mahila convoys are extra, but as they take several weeks to do the journey their help is limited.

I have just seen the padre who has been working in the field dressing station. In his station there were two doctors, two nursing orderlies and two native sweepers; and these had to cope with 750 white wounded for five days till they could ship them down the river. Altogether our casualties in the two battles have been well over 5,000, so the Turk has rather scored.

This afternoon news is () that we have got a new Brigadier. Our brigade manages its commanders on the principle of the caliph and his wives, and has not yet found a Sherazade. () that we have got a brigade M.O.O. ambulance. This is a luxury indeed. We are only just over twenty miles from C. now, so we hope to get through after one more battle.

16th, Sunday. Still in camp. No sun. More rain. Friday's gale and the rise in the river has scattered our only pontoon bridge, and Heaven knows when another will be ready. All our skilled bridge-builders are in C. The people here seem quite incapable of even bridging the Canal, twenty feet wide. Typical, very.

I want a new shaving brush—badger's hair, not too large.

Mail just going. Best love.

P.S.—We had a Celebration on a boat this morning, which I was very glad of, also a voluntary parade service.

Last letter from R.P. to L. Palmer giving story from January 12th to January 21st.

I wrote you last week a summary of our doings during the battle of D. Now I will tell you what we have done since, though it is mostly unpleasant.

The evening after I posted last week's letter "D." Coy. had to find a firing party to shoot a havildar, a lance-naik and a sepoy for cowardice in face of the enemy. Thank goodness North and not I was detailed for it. They helped dig their own graves and were very brave about it. They lay down in the graves to be shot. Corp. Boughey was one of the party and when I condoled with him afterwards on the unpleasantness of the job, he replied, "Well, Sir, I 'ad a bit of rust in my barrel wanted shootin' out so it come in handy like"!

Thursday, 13th. We marched at 7 carrying food and water for two days. We were in support of the frontal containing force. The enemy were on the Canal, eight miles off. We marched about four miles and then halted, and waited most of the day for orders. A strong S.E. wind prevented us hearing anything of the battle but we could see a certain amount of shelling. About 3 p.m. we got orders to go up in support of the frontal force, which (we were told) had advanced, the enemy having abandoned the Canal. We marched another three miles to a fort, which stood about one and a quarter miles from the Canal, and from which we had driven the enemy in the morning. Here we waited till after dark, when we heard that the frontal force had blundered into a Turkish rearguard holding the Canal, and had lost heavily and been obliged to retire. It is these disconcerting surprises which try one's spirit more than anything else. We ate a cold and cheerless supper just beyond the fort, and then dug ourselves in, with other units of our brigade on either side of us. It was windy and very cold. There was a small and filthy hut with every mark of recent Turkish use, just behind the trench, but sooner or later every officer (I among the first) came to the conclusion that dirt was preferable to cold, and we all packed in round a fire which our signallers had lit there.

Friday, 14th. After a tolerable night we stood to arms at 5.30, a wholly displeasing process. As soon as it was light, we advanced to within 1,200 yds. of the Canal and started digging in. But it soon became clear that the enemy had cleared out in the night, so we stopped digging and started to clear up the battlefield, *i.e.*, the space between us and the Canal. The stretcher parties had been out during the night, but they had been fired on so heavily that they could not get beyond the 1,200 yd. line, so there were wounded to pick up as well as dead to bury and equipment to collect. The dead were so pitiable that one quite forgot their ghastliness; but it was a gruesome job searching their pockets. The poor wounded had had a fearful time too, lying out in the cold all night, but the satisfaction of getting them in cheered one up. The ground was simply littered with pointed bullets.

In the middle of this job we were recalled and told to march to the support of our outflanking force; but by the time we were collected and fallen in the need for our assistance had apparently passed, for we were merely marched to the Canal and then along it to where it joins the river; where we have been ever since. We got into camp here soon after noon, and were very glad to be within reach of water again. The weather was the limit. It blew a gale all the afternoon, and the dust was so bad one could hardly open one's eyes. We had no tents, but the Major (Stilwell) had a bivouac and invited me in with him, which was a blessing as it rained all night.

Saturday, 15th. Rained all the morning on and off. Afternoon grey and cold. Nothing doing and no news. Sniping at night.

Sunday, 16th. Morning grey and cold. Rained all the afternoon and is still at it (8 p.m.). Padre held a celebration on one of the boats, and an open air voluntary parade service. Dug a bridge-head perimetre. We are waiting for the bridge. The gale and the river bust it.

Monday, 17th. Rained on and off all day. Grey, cold and windy. Ordered to cross river as soon as bridge is ready. Bridge reported ready 6 p.m. so we struck camp.

We took only what blankets we could carry. When we reached the bridge, we found it not finished, and squatted till 8.15. Then the bridge was finished and immediately broke. So we had to come back to camp and bivouac. Luckily the officers tents were recoverable, but not the men's.

Tuesday, 18th. Rain stopped at 8 a.m. Whole place a sea of mud ankle deep, and slippery as butter. Nearly the whole bridge had been washed away or sunk in the night. We got men's tents from the ship, cleared spaces from mud and pitched camp again. Rain started again about 1 p.m. and continued till 4. The Canal or "Wadi" had meanwhile come down in heavy spate and broken that bridge, so we were doubly isolated. I went out to post piquets. It took two hours to walk three miles. Jubber Khan sick all day, so I had to manage for myself, helped by North's bearer. Foster being sick North is O.C. "D." Coy. and I share a 40lb. tent with him. He is 2/4th, son of the Duke of Wellington's Agent at Strathfieldsaye, but has served three years in N. Rhodesia, so is quite used to camp life.

Desultory bombardment all day.

Wednesday 19th. Sun at last; first fine day since Thursday last. Orders to cross Wadi as soon as bridge repaired. Crossed at 4 p.m. and camped in a dry place.

Thursday, 20th. Fair, sun, heavy bombardment all day. Post going.

Account of Fighting which took Place in the Attack on
the Turkish Position of Um el Hanna, on January 21st, 1916.

By an Officer who was There.

The Turkish position, which is about ten miles up stream from Shaikh Saad, is on the left bank of the Tigris. The position is a very strong one, thoroughly entrenched, with the river protecting its right flank and absolutely secured on its left flank by a very extensive marsh which stretches for miles.

Our camp was about five miles from the Turkish position (downstream) but our forward trenches were within about 1,000 yards of it.

On January 20th our guns bombarded the enemy's trenches at intervals during the day, and on the following morning at 3 a.m. we moved out of camp preparatory to the attack which was to commence about 6.30 a.m.

The —— Brigade was to push the main attack with the —— Brigade (ours) in support of it, whilst a third brigade was to make a holding attack on our right.

The leading brigade entrenched itself during the night within about 500 yards of the position, whilst our Regiment with one Indian Regiment formed the first line of supports. We were in our trenches about 1,000 yards from the enemy's position, ready to make the attack, by 6 a.m.

For some reason, which I do not know, the attack was delayed, and our guns did not open fire till 7.45 a.m. instead of 6.30 as originally intended.

At 7.55 a.m. after our guns had bombarded the enemy's trenches for only ten minutes the infantry were ordered to advance to the attack, our support line advancing at the same time.

Our Battalion, which consisted of three Companies (one Coy. being in Kut-el-Amara) advanced in three lines, "B" Coy. forming the first line under Lieut.

Needham, "C" Coy. the second line under Capt. Page Roberts, and "D" Coy. the third line under Capt. North with Capt. the Hon. R. Palmer as his 2nd in command. Lt.-Col. Bowker was with the third line.

As soon as we left the trenches we were under a heavy rifle fire, and as we advanced this became more and more intense, with machine gun and shrapnel fire added. The ground was perfectly flat and open with no form of cover to be obtained, and our casualties soon became very heavy. We continued to advance till we got to within about 150 yards of the enemy's trenches, but by this time our casualties were so heavy that it was impossible to press home the attack without reinforcements, though at the extreme left of our line, our troops actually got into the first line of trenches, but were bombed out of them again by the Turks.

No reinforcements reached us, however, and we afterwards heard that the Regiment which should have come up in support of us was enfiladed from their right and was consequently drawn off in that direction. All we could do now was to hold on where we were, making what cover we could with our entrenching tools, and this we did until darkness came on, when we withdrew.

The weather had been terrible all that day and night, there being heavy rain with a bitterly cold wind coming off the snow hills. The ground became a sea of mud which made it most difficult to remove the wounded, and many of these had to lie out till the armistice was arranged the following day.

Further Descriptions of the Fight at Um el Hanna, By Eye-Witnesses.

By an Officer of the 4th Hants.

"The fighting on the 21st was a pure slaughter. It was too awful....

"The troops from France say that in all their experience there they never suffered so much from weather conditions.

"We were wet to the skin and there was a bitter wind coming off the snow hills. Many poor fellows died from exposure that night, I am afraid; and many of the wounded were lying out for more than twenty-four hours until the armistice was arranged the following day."

Another written down from a Private's account.

"The three Companies of Hampshires were in support, with two native Regiments, and a Battalion of Connaught Rangers. The Black Watch and Seaforths were in the firing line. The Hants men were next the river. The two native Regiments refused to leave their trenches when they saw the fierce fire from the machine guns. The Connaughts were fighting further off. So the Hampshire men were obliged to go on alone. 'We never made a rush, and just walked slowly through the rain. A slow march to our deaths, I call it.'"

He then said they had got mixed up with the Black Watch and got into the first Turkish trench, but had been driven out of it again. He saw Capt. Palmer fall about 200 yards from the trench but did not see whether he got up again, or where he was wounded.

Thornfield,
Bitterne,
Southampton,

10th August, 1916.

Dear Lady Selborne,

I have just received a letter from 2nd Lt. C.H. Vernon, 1/4 Hants (really 2/7 Hants attached) recording his search for my son's body on the 7th April, 1916, its discovery (as he believes) and its burial. He also adds that "at the same time he looked for Capt. Palmer's, but could not find him. It was afterwards that he heard of his death in the Turkish Camp," and he adds, "Some stories have come through from survivors as to how he lost his life. As far as we can gather, he was the only Hants officer actually to penetrate the Turkish trenches with a few men. That was on the extreme left close to the river. Our men, however, had not been supplied by the Indian Government with bombs. Consequently the Turks, being so provided, bombed them out, and only one or two men escaped capture or death. It was here that Capt. Palmer was mortally wounded while trying to rally his men to hold the captured sector."

I think you may like to have this extract about your gallant son.

(*Signed*) J.T. Bucknill.

42, Pall Mall,
London, S.W.

8th March, 1916.

The Hampshires were informed that another Battalion was in front of them, and advanced without returning the hostile fire till they got to 1,000 yards from the Turkish trenches—they then found out that there were no British troops in front, so opened fire and advanced. The Connaught Rangers on their right remained behind when they found out the mistake. Two native Battalions in reserve refused to budge, although their officers threatened them with their revolvers. The artillery preparation proved insufficient, but the Hampshires got into shell holes and held on till dark. The medical arrangements broke down, there were insufficient stretcher-bearers, and no chloroform or sufficient bandages. No mention is made of the Arabs, however.

There were seventy-five rank and file returned as missing after the fight, and a subaltern, Lieut. Lester Garland, took over the command of the Battalion when my brother collapsed.

The Turks claimed to have captured five officers in one action, but there is so much "fog of war" in those parts that it is difficult to identify their claims.

(*Signed*) G.H. Stilwell.

42, Pall Mall.
London, S.W.

1st May, 1916.

At the armistice to collect the wounded it was agreed that all officers and men that fell within 200 yards of the Turkish trenches should be picked up and retained by the Turks as prisoners, while all beyond that zone should be removed by us. Your son was seen within 100 yards of the Turkish trench when he fell, and it was reported that four of his men actually got inside the trench, but were driven out by bombs. My son was with the next platoon to yours, and Bucknill was a little further on. They were obviously well in front, and fell in the enemy's zone.

(*Signed*) G.H. Stilwell.

1/4th Hampshire Regiment,
I.E.F. "D,"
C/o India Office, S.W.

20th February, 1916.

I received your cable enquiring about your son to-day, and have wired to the Adjutant General at the base at Basra enquiring whether he has any information not known to the Regiment, as I very much regret to say we have none whatever. All we know is that he started in the attack on the Turkish trenches on the 21st January and has not been seen since. I write to-day as the mail is leaving, but will cable as soon as I get a reply from the base. Out of 310 who went into the attack we had 288 casualties. Bucknill and a good many men are missing as well. There was great difficulty in getting the wounded back as it had to be done at night and the rain and mud were appalling.

There was an armistice next day, but we were not allowed to go within a certain distance of the Turkish trenches, so all wounded within that area are probably prisoners.

One other officer of ours was captured and we only found that out incidentally. There has been no official list of prisoners and I don't think the Army

Headquarters here know who was taken. I don't know whether you would have the means of getting this from the Turks through the War Office. I believe attempts are being made here. I think there is a chance of his being a prisoner as the Regiment got pretty near the trenches, but I can get no information from any of our men. I will cable at once if I hear anything.

I saw yesterday a copy of the *Pioneer* (Allahabad) for January 30th, and that reported your son wounded. I hoped, therefore, that he had been sent to India and the medical people in this country had omitted to make any record of it, but I imagine in that case he would surely have cabled to you himself, and I fear the only hope is that he may be a prisoner of war.

Your son was attached to my Company latterly and besides being very keen and capable was a great favourite with the men, and we all miss him very much indeed. I hope your Lordship will accept my deepest sympathy in your anxiety, and I sincerely hope that your son may be safe.

(*Signed*) H.M. Foster,
Capt. 1/4th Hants Regt.

H.M.S. "Mantis,"

May, 1916.

Dear Lord Selborne.

I am more grieved than I can say to have given you the news which I telegraphed yesterday. I know how cruel the anxiety of doubt is, and telegraphed to you when I had the evidence which I and my friends here considered reliable.

About six days ago I went out to the Turks to discuss terms for the surrender of Kut. I spent the night in their camp and have been with them several times since then. I asked them for information about three names. About two of the names I could get little information. On the third day I received a message from Ali Jenab Bey, telling me that your son had died in hospital, and that all that could be done for him had been done, and asking me to tell you how deeply he sympathised with you. The next day Ali Jenab and two other Turks came into our camp. One of them, Mohammed Riza, a relation of Jenab Pashas, told me that your son had been brought in after the fight on the 21st, slightly wounded in the shoulder and badly wounded in the chest. He had been well looked after by the Doctors and the Colonel of the Regiment (I could not find out which Regiment) had visited him, and at the Doctor's wish sent him some brandy. He did not suffer and the end came after four hours.

It is useless to try to tell you how sorry I feel for you and all of yours. In this campaign, which in my mind has been the most heroic of all, many of our men who have given their lives have suffered very long and very terribly, and when one hears of a friend who has gone, one is glad in this place, to know that he has been spared that sacrifice.

I am,
Yours very sincerely,

(*Signed*) Aubrey Herbert.

APPENDIX I.

The Official Account of the Battle taken from Sir Percy Lake's Despatch to the War Office, published October, 1916.

It will be noticed that it differs from the private accounts in one or two particulars.

1st phase—January 19—23.

After the battle of Wadi River General Aylmer's leading troops had followed the retreating Turks to the Umm-el-Hannah position, and entrenched themselves at the mouth of the defile, so as to shut the enemy in and limit his power of taking the offensive.

The weather at this period was extraordinarily unfavourable. Heavy rains caused the river to come down in flood and overflow its banks, and converted the ground on either bank into a veritable bog.

Our bridge across the Wadi was washed away several times, while the boisterous winds greatly interfered with the construction of a bridge across the Tigris, here some 400 yards in width.

It was essential to establish Artillery on the right bank of the Tigris, so as to support, by enfilading fire, the attack of our Infantry against the Hannah position.

Guns and troops were ferried across, with difficulty, owing to the high wind and heavy squalls of rain, but by the 19th all troops allotted to the right bank had crossed over and were established in the positions from which they were required to co-operate with the main force on the left bank.

Meanwhile, the leading Infantry Brigades on the left bank had pushed nearer the enemy. January 20th was devoted to a systematic bombardment of his position, and during the night the Infantry pushed forward their advanced line to within 200 yards of the enemy's trenches.

On the morning of the 21st, under cover of an intensive Artillery bombardment, our Infantry moved to the attack. On our right the troops got to within 100 yards of the enemy's line, but were unable to advance further. Our left column, consisting of the Black Watch, 6th Jats, and 41st Dogras, penetrated the front line with a rush, capturing trenches, which they held for about an hour and a half. Supports were sent forward, but, losing direction and coming under heavy fire, failed to reach them. Thus, left unsupported, our previously successful troops, when Turkish counter-attacks developed, were overwhelmed by numbers and forced to retire.

Heavy rain now began to fall and continued throughout the day. Telephone communication broke down, and communication by orderly became slow and uncertain.

After further artillery bombardment the attack was renewed at 1 p.m., but by this time the heavy rain had converted the ground into a sea of mud, rendering rapid movement impossible. The enemy's fire was heavy and effective, inflicting severe losses, and though every effort was made, the assault failed.

Our troops maintained their position until dark and then slowly withdrew to the main trenches which had been previously occupied, some 1,300 yards from those of the enemy.

As far as possible all the wounded were brought in during the withdrawal, but their sufferings and hardships were acute under the existing climatic conditions, when vehicles and stretcher-bearers could scarcely move in the deep mud.

To renew the attack on the 22nd was not practicable. The losses on the 21st had been heavy, the ground was still a quagmire and the troops exhausted. A six hours' armistice was arranged in order to bury the dead and remove the wounded to shelter.

I cannot sufficiently express my admiration for the courage and dogged determination of the force engaged. For days they bivouacked in driving rain on soaked and sodden ground. Three times they were called upon to advance over a perfectly flat country, deep in mud, and absolutely devoid of cover, against well-constructed and well-planned trenches, manned by a brave and stubborn enemy approximately their equal in numbers. They showed a spirit of endurance and self-sacrifice of which their country may well be proud.

APPENDIX II.

Extracts from Letters from Officers and Men of the 6th Hants.

Your son was universally liked and respected by all ranks in this Battalion, and one and all will regret his death and loss as much as I do, who knew his sterling worth. His memory will be ever cherished by his brother officers with whom he was so popular.

(*Signed*) F.H. Playfair, *Col.*

I was indeed sorry to receive your letter which my brother sent on to me, giving the news of your son's death from his wounds in the Turkish trenches. I had great hopes that his wound might have been a slight one.

May I offer Lady Selborne and yourself the most sincere sympathy both of the Regiment and myself in this most sad loss which has come to you. I can assure you both officers and men of the Regiment will miss him tremendously as he was so popular with all.

(*Signed*) W. B. Stilwell, *Major.*

---- shewed me the wire about Robert yesterday morning. I can't tell you how sorry I feel for you all. I know I have never lost anyone who meant anything like so much to me, and I am sure that his friendship was one of the greatest blessings for me, in every way, that God could have given me.

When a fellow not only has such ideals but actually lives up to them with the determination and consistency with which Robert did, I think there is something very triumphant about his life. Anyway I know that his influence will live on, not in his friends alone, but in everyone with whom he came in contact. I wish you could know what a tremendous lot people thought of him in the Regiment, both officers and men, some of whom had little in common with him.

With deepest sympathy for you all.

Yours very sincerely,
(*Signed*) Purefoy Causton.

From a Private Soldier.

I had only seen that Robert Palmer had been wounded;

the issue giving the subsequent and very terrible report had escaped me. I am more sorry than I can well express. Though I didn't know him personally yet it didn't take long to recognise him as one of the great strengths in the Battalion, it was noticeable from the very first, from the way he handled his Company and went about working for them—on the "Ultonia" it struck me.

Extracts from Letters from School and College Friends.

Accept my most grateful thanks for your kind words of sympathy. As you say, this war, with all its terrible consequences, "had to be," and it is some comfort to us to know that our sons, meant for other things than violence, took their part in it serenely and cheerfully, with no misgivings.

I often think of your dear boy and of what he said about the war in that sonnet. But what I most often think of him, as I can of my own son, is "Blessed are the pure in heart."

(*Signed*) A.K. Cook.

I had looked forward myself to a great career for him: he had so many qualities to ensure success: a sharp, keen mind, which proved its literary quality also at Oxford, an unfailing earnestness and high purpose and a white character: no one could deny the brilliance and the steadiness of his gifts.

(*Signed*) M.J. Rendall.

I have just received the "Wykehamist War Roll" and *The Wykehamist* and in it find the sad news of your boy. I did not know definite news had been received and was still hoping. May I add my letter of sympathy to the many you will have had from all his friends, for though sympathy does not do much good it does sometimes help a little I believe, and say how very, very much I feel for you and Lady Selborne in your loss. He was my senior prefect my first year at "Cook's," and there never was a kinder, fairer and more liked prefect by the small boys all the time I was there, and indeed I think I have never met a better fellow anywhere.

(*Signed*) F. Luttman-Johnson.

I have only just learned from the announcement in to-day's papers that you have no longer any ground for hoping against hope. I did not mean to write to you, but the sense of the loss and of how England will miss him in the years to come has been so strongly in my mind all day that I thought perhaps you would not mind my trying to put it into words. I did not see very much of him, but I have never forgotten the first impression of him that I got as external examiner at Winchester, when he was in Sixth Book and how I felt he was marked out for big work, and I had always looked forward to getting to know him better. It makes one feel very, very old when those on whom one relied to carry on one's work and ideas are taken. But it is a happiness—or at least a sort of shining consolation—to think that one will always remember him as radiantly young. I have lost so many pupils who will never grow up and always be just pupils.

Please do not think of replying and pardon this intrusion.

(*Signed*) A. Zimmern.

Bobby was gold all through—for head and heart one in a million. Of all the undergraduates I have known at Oxford during my twenty years of work there, he struck me as most certain by reason of his breadth and sobriety of judgment, intellectual force and sweetness of disposition to exercise a commanding influence for good in the public affairs of the country. Everyone admired and liked him and I know that his influence among his contemporaries, an influence exercised very quietly and unobtrusively, was quite exceptional from the very first.

(*Signed*) Herbert Fisher.

Those of us who knew Bobby at Univ. and saw him afterwards in London knew that one way or another he would give his life to the country. The war has only determined the manner of his giving and made the life much shorter, but his memory the more abiding.

(*Signed*) Alec Paterson, *2nd Lieut.*

Frontispiece. *British troops going on picket -- Mesopotamia*
[Photograph] At:
http://www.gwpda.org/photos/coppermine/displayimage
.php?album=search&cat=0&pos=3

Lightning Source UK Ltd.
Milton Keynes UK
UKOW02f0822200916

283395UK00004B/109/P